Lonely Planet Kids

HIDDEN WONDERS

DISCOVER OUR PLANET'S BEST-KEPT SECRETS

NICOLE MAGGI AND KATE BAKER

CONT

INTRODUCTION
PAGE **6**

LONGITUDE -180°/-120°
PAGE **8**

Discover
disappearing islands and the world's largest maze

LONGITUDE -120°/-60°
PAGE **28**

Encounter
a cave of giant crystals and a museum filled with brains

LONGITUDE -60°/0°
PAGE **74**

Find
an island teeming with snakes and an underground railway

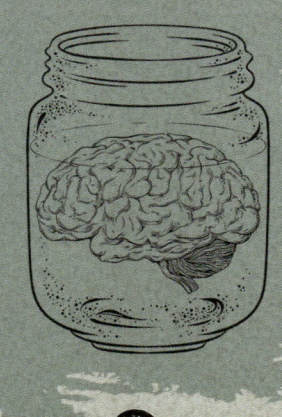

ENTS

LONGITUDE 0°/60°

PAGE 100

Stroll
through a grove of curved trees and witness a volcano spewing lava

LONGITUDE 60°/120°

PAGE 156

Uncover
ancient city ruins and hang out with thousands of garden gnomes

LONGITUDE 120°/180°

PAGE 192

Witness
coffins clinging to a cliffside and caves illuminated by glowworms

INDEX

PAGE 234

6   Introduction

8   Longitude –180° / –120°

10 Waitavala Waterslide, Taveuni, Fiji
11 Hunga Tonga-Hunga Ha'Apai, Tonga
12 Aniakchak National Monument & Preserve, Alaska, USA
14 Pineapple Garden Maze, Oahu, Hawaii, USA
15 Kiritimati, Kiribati
16 Pu'Upiha Cemetery, Maui, Hawaii, USA
17 Rainbow Eucalyptus Trees, Maui, Hawaii, USA
18 Papakōlea Beach, Maui, Hawaii, USA
19 Spirit Houses, Eklutna, Alaska, USA
20 The Felled Golden Spruce, British Columbia, Canada
22 California's Lost Coast, California, USA
23 Mammoth Rubbing Rocks, California, USA
24 Whistler Train Wreck Site, British Columbia, Canada
25 The Wave Organ, San Francisco, California, USA
26 The Giant Pumpkin Regatta, Tualatin, Oregon, USA
27 Winchester Mystery House, San Jose, California, USA

28 Longitude –120° / –60°

30 Spotted Lake, Osoyoos, British Columbia, Canada
31 Fly Ranch Geyser, Nevada, USA
32 The Shoe Tree, Highway 50, Nevada, USA
33 Racetrack Playa, Death Valley National Park, California, USA
34 Blythe Geoglyphs, Blythe, California, USA
35 Nine Mile Canyon, Utah, USA
36 The Navel of the World, Easter Island, Chile
37 Hidden Beach, Marieta Islands, Mexico
38 Cave of the Crystals, Chihuahua, Mexico
40 The Polar Bear Capital of the World, Churchill, Manitoba, Canada
42 Wichita Mountains Wildlife Refuge, Indiahoma, Oklahoma, USA
43 Actun Tunichil Muknal, Cayo, Belize
44 Old Car City, White, Georgia, USA
45 Parque Francisco Alvarado, Costa Rica
46 Tank Town USA, Georgia, USA
47 Diquís Spheres, Diquís Delta, Costa Rica
48 Fusterlandia, Havana, Cuba
50 Hell, Grand Cayman, Cayman Islands
51 Coral Castle, Near Miami, Florida, USA
52 The Swing at the End of the World, Tungurahua Province, Ecuador
53 Museo del Cerebro, Lima, Peru
54 Pig Beach, Big Major Cay, The Bahamas
55 La Cueva del Esplendor, Colombia
56 El Peñón de Guatapé, Colombia
57 Nazca Lines, Nazca Desert, Peru
58 Catedral de Sal, Zipaquirá, Colombia
59 Sleepy Hollow Cemetery, New York, USA
60 Cueva del Milodón Natural Monument, Patagonia, Chile
61 Moray, Miras, Peru
62 Dock of Souls, Chiloé, Chile
64 Q-Eswachaka Rope Bridge, Canas, Peru
65 Witches' Market, La Paz, Bolivia
66 Cementerio de Trenes, Uyuni, Bolivia
67 Tanks of Flamenco Beach, Culebra, Puerto Rico (USA)
68 Parque Cretácico, Sucre, Bolivia
69 Tektite Underwater Habitat, Virgin Islands (USA)
70 Soufrière Hills Volcano, Montserrat (UK)
72 The Moonhole, Bequia, St Vincent & the Grenadines
73 Deception Island, Antarctica

74 Longitude –60° / 0°

76 Gruta do Lago Azul, Bonito, Brazil
77 L'Anse Aux Meadows, Island's Bay, Newfoundland and Labrador, Canada
78 Vale da Lua, Alto Paraíso de Goiás, Brazil
79 Snake Island (Ilha da Queimada Grande), Brazil
80 Parque Nacinal Dos Lençóis Maranhenses, Maranhão, Brazil
82 Rock Paintings of Parque Nacional Serra de Capivara, Piauí, Brazil
83 Blue Ice Caves, Vatnajökull National Park, Iceland
84 Senegambian Stone Circles, Senegal and Gamibia
85 Fairy Forts, Ireland
86 Fingal's Cave, Staffa Island, Scotland, UK
88 Chouara Leather Tannery, Fez, Morocco
90 Playa de Gulpiyuri, Near Llanes, Spain
91 Submerged Forest, Ceredigon, Wales, UK
92 Grande Mosquée, Djenné, Mali
94 The Kelpies, Falkirk, Scotland, UK
95 Cliff Dwellings of the Bandiagara, Bandiagara Escarpment, Mali
96 Antogo Fishing Frenzy, Koro, Mali
97 Kane Kwei Coffins, Accra, Ghana
98 The Mail Rail, London, England, UK

100 Longitude 0° / 60°

- 102 Les Grottes Pétrifiantes, France
- 103 Egungun Vodún Ceremony, Cove, Benin
- 104 Catacombes de Paris, Paris, France
- 106 Osun Sacred Forest, Osogbo, Nigeria
- 107 Le Palais Idéal, Hauterives, France
- 108 Kjeragbolten, Øygardstøl, Norway
- 109 Trolltunga, Near Tyssedal, Norway
- 110 Miniatur Wunderland, Hamburg, Germany
- 111 Campanile di Curon, South Tyrol, Italy
- 112 Triftbrücke, The Alps, Switzerland
- 113 Tollund Man, Silkeborg, Denmark
- 114 Råbjerg Mile, Near Skagen, Denmark
- 116 Colosseum Hypogeum, Rome, Italy
- 117 Passetto di Borgo, Rome, Italy
- 118 The Sunken City of Baiae, Gulf of Puteolo, Italy
- 119 Crooked Forest, Poland
- 120 Želizy Devil Heads, Želizy, Czechia
- 121 Plitvice Lakes National Park, Croatia
- 122 Postojna Caves, Postojna, Slovenia
- 124 Stromboli, Near Sicily, Italy
- 125 Wild Horses of the Namib Desert, Namibia
- 126 Global Seed Vault, Svalbard, Norway
- 128 Wolfberg Arch, Central Cederberg, South Africa
- 129 Drina River House, Bajina Bašta, Serbia
- 130 Witches' Hill, Juodkrante, Lithuania
- 131 Kaleto Fortress, Belogradchik, Bulgaria
- 132 Stob Pyramids, Stob, Bulgaria
- 133 Hill of Crosses, Near Šiauliai, Lithuania
- 134 Owl House, Nieu-Bethesda, South Africa
- 135 Kubu Island, Makgadikgadi Pan, Botswana
- 136 Living Fires, Lopatari, Romania
- 137 Kummakivi, Ruokolahti, Finland
- 138 Matobo National Park, Matobo, Zimbabwe
- 140 Pamukkale-Hierapolis, Denizli, Turkey
- 141 Nyiragongo, Virunga Mountains, Democratic Republic of Congo
- 142 Bat Migration, Zambia
- 144 Wadi Al-Hitan (Whale Valley), White Desert, Faiyum, Egypt
- 145 Pyramids of Meroë, River Nile State, Sudan
- 146 Derinkuyu, Cappadocia, Turkey
- 148 The Forest of Knives, Tsingy de Bemaraha National Park, Madagascar
- 149 Pigeon Towers, Iran
- 150 Dragon Blood Trees, Socotra, Yemen
- 152 Zoroastrian Towers of Silence, Yazd, Iran
- 153 Bat & Al Ayn Tombs, Bat, Oman
- 154 Darvaza Gas Crater, Karakum Desert, Turkmenistan

156 Longitude 60° / 120°

- 158 Princess of Hope, Hingol National Park, Pakistan
- 159 Bayterek Monument, Astana, Kazakhstan
- 160 Karni Mata Temple, Bikaner, India
- 161 The Sea of Stars, The Maldives
- 162 Singing Dunes of Altyn-Emel National Park, Almaty Region, Kazakhstan
- 163 Lake Kaindy, Kolsai Lakes National Park, Kazakhstan
- 164 Meghalaya Tree Bridges, Bikaner, India
- 165 Kyaiktiyo Pagoda, Mon State, Myanmar (Burma)
- 166 Rainbow Mountains, Zhangye Danxia National Geopark, China
- 168 Arulmigu Sri Rajakaliamman, Malaysia
- 169 Flaming Cliffs, Gobi Desert, Mongolia
- 170 Fuxian Lake, Yunnan Province, China
- 172 Haw Par Villa, Singapore
- 173 Temple of Ta Prohm, Siem Reap, Cambodia
- 174 Creepy-Crawly Markets, Bangkok, Thailand
- 176 Kbal Spean, Near Siem Reap, Cambodia
- 177 Olkhon Island, Siberia, Russia
- 178 Red Crab Migration, Christmas Island, Australia
- 180 Gunung Padang, Karyamukti, Indonesia
- 181 Am Phu Cave, Near Da Nang, Vietnam
- 182 My Son, Near Hoi An, Vietnam
- 184 Gereja Ayam, Near Magelang, Indonesia
- 186 Zhengbel Tower, Near Beijing, China
- 187 Longyou Caves, Zhejiang Province, China
- 188 Gnomesville, Western Australia, Australia
- 190 Rafflesia Flower, Kalimantan, Borneo, Indonesia
- 191 Komodo Dragons, Komodo National Park, Indonesia

192 Longitude 120° / 180°

- 194 Echo Valley Hanging Coffins, Sagada, Philippines
- 195 Lake Ballard, Western Australia, Australia
- 196 Lake Hillier, Western Australia, Australia
- 198 Rainbow Village, Taichung, Taiwan
- 199 Beneficial Microbes Museum, Yilan, Taiwan
- 200 Houtouwan, Shengshan Island, China
- 201 Nara Park, Nara, Japan
- 202 Haenyeo, Jeju Island, South Korea
- 203 Star-Sand Beaches, Iriomote Island, Japan
- 204 Heaven Lake, China and North Korea
- 205 North Korean Submarine, South Korea
- 206 Jellyfish Lake, Eil Malk Island, Palau
- 208 Coober Pedy, South Australia, Australia
- 210 Injalak Hill, West Arnhem Land, Northern Territory, Australia
- 211 Garma Festival, East Arnhem Land, Northern Territory, Australia
- 212 Rai Stones, Yap, Micronesia
- 213 Korowai Tree Houses, Papua, Indonesia
- 214 Jigokudani Monkey Park, Joshinetsu Kogen National Park, Japan
- 216 Cat Island, Tashirojima, Japan
- 217 Giant Pink Slugs of Mt Kaputar, New South Wales, Australia
- 218 SS *Ayrfield*, New South Wales, Australia
- 220 Valley of Geysers, Kamchatka Peninsula, Russia
- 221 Heart of Voh, Grande Terre, New Caledonia
- 222 Underwater Post Office, Hideaway Island, Vanuatu
- 223 Slope Point, Southland District, New Zealand
- 224 Land Divers of Pentecost Island, Pentecost Island, Vanuatu
- 226 Baldwin Street, Dunedin, New Zealand
- 227 Wildfoods Festival, Hokitika, New Zealand
- 228 Kāpiti Island Nature Reserve, New Zealand
- 229 Champagne Pool, Wai-O-Tapu, New Zealand
- 230 Waitomo Glowworm Caves, Waitomo, New Zealand
- 232 Taumatawhakata-Tangihangakoau-Auotamateaturi Pukakapikimaun-Gahoronukupokai-Whenuakitanatahu, Hawke's Bay, New Zealand

234 Index

The Swing at the End of the World, Ecuador (see page 52)

INTRODUCTION

Oh, wondrous discovery! You hold in your hands the shining key to some of the world's most secret places. Grab your compass and travel to the far reaches of this glorious planet. Descend into caves lit by glow-worms brighter than the brightest chandelier. Uncover ancient history beneath the waves. Float on waters as pink as a rose, swim with wild pigs on a pristine beach, and fly over the mouth of a volcano on the world's most daring swing.

Will you discover mermaids on a tiny island in South Korea, or witches deep in a Lithuanian forest? This book will take you everywhere and beyond. Each section includes all of the fascinating destinations you'll find at a specific line of longitude, those imaginary lines that divide the globe vertically and meet up at the North and South Poles.

So get ready to stand on the edge of a fiery crater or lose yourself in the world's largest maze. Whether deep underwater in a prehistoric grotto or high on a cliff at the tip of a rock troll's tongue, adventure awaits around every corner. You have only to turn the page to discover it!

Trek to the spot of a famous felled tree p20

LONGITUDE -180°/-120°

Go off the beaten track along California's Lost Coast p22

Enter a miniature world for the dead p19

Uncover street art
and train wrecks in the middle of a forest p24

Be amazed
by rainbow trees painted by nature p17

Bob along
in a pumpkin boat p26

TAVEUNI, FIJI

WAITAVALA WATER SLIDE

LONGITUDE -180°/-120°

Surf down on your feet or slide down on your bottom. Whichever you choose, you'll whizz through the beautiful rainforest with surprising speed when you take a ride on the Waitavala water slide. Formed completely by natural forces, this fierce, slippery slope takes you down a chute along smooth rock formations in the jungles of Fiji. Your favourite water park's got nothing on this thrill ride.

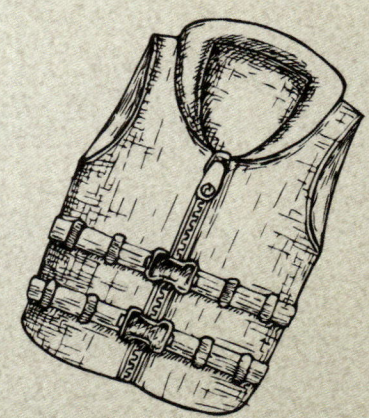

TONGA
HUNGA TONGA-HUNGA HA'APAI

The island shown before (above) and after (below) the 2022 eruption – the yellow line marks its former extent.

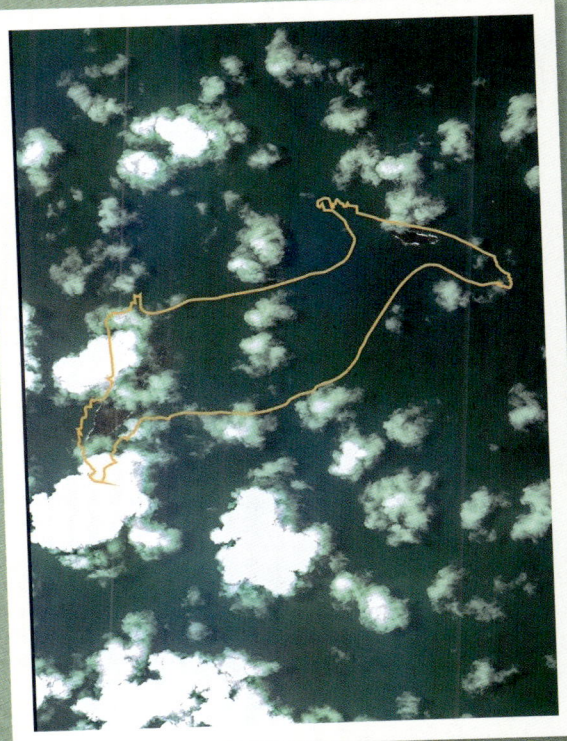

This shape-shifting island began life as an undersea volcano until 2015, when it burst out of the Pacific Ocean. The ash plumes from the eruption were so vast they diverted flights for days. When it settled down, it formed a seahorse-shaped island with a milky green lake in the middle of its crater. However, on 15 January 2022, an enormous volcanic eruption – the largest of the 21st century so far – caused much of the young island to retreat once more beneath the waves. All that was left were two small volcanic islands, Hunga Tonga and Hunga Ha'apai, marking the remains of the northern and western rim of the volcano. Despite their turbulent past, the islands continue to support a surprising variety of life, including guava trees, sooty terns and other seabirds, rats, spiders and hermit crabs, while humpback whales, sea snakes and sharks swim in the surrounding waters.

LONGITUDE -180°/-120°

ALASKA, USA

ANIAKCHAK NATIONAL MONUMENT & PRESERVE

LONGITUDE -180°/-120°

More people explore space each year than visit the otherworldly Aniakchak National Monument and Preserve. A collapsed volcanic crater, this barren landscape feels more than a little like a 'lost world'. Giant grizzly bears wander across the tundra. Clouds fill up the crater and spill over the edges like waterfalls. Only the most intrepid explorers hike down into the crater, using animal trails, before whitewater rafting down the Aniakchak River out to Aniakchak Bay and the Pacific Ocean.

OAHU, HAWAII, USA
PINEAPPLE GARDEN MAZE

It's not hard to get lost in this labyrinth, which was twice named the World's Largest Maze by Guinness World Records. It covers an area of more than 12,000 sq m (130,000 sq ft) and is built entirely out of plants found in Hawaii.

Race through hibiscus, panax and pineapple plants to see if you can beat the fastest time recorded (seven minutes). Most people take about 45 minutes to complete the maze, but why rush when you're surrounded by all this beauty?

LONGITUDE -180°/-120°

KIRIBATI

KIRITIMATI

When the British explorer Captain James Cook landed here on Christmas Day in 1777, he named the island Christmas Island. In the local language it is Kiritimati, pronounced 'Krismas' because the 'ti' sounds like an 's' in English. The island is the world's biggest coral atoll and is so remote, it's populated with more birds than people. Here you can visit London, Paris, and Poland without even buying a plane ticket. Those are the names of three of the island's four early settlements. The island was a former British colony, so the name London makes sense. As for Paris and Poland? The French owner of a coconut plantation named them for his home country, and the home of his Polish engineer. The fourth settlement? It's called Banana – possibly because it was the site of the island's first banana groves!

LONGITUDE -180°/-120°

Kiritimati is just one of 33 islands that make up the country of Kirbati (pronounced 'Ki-ree-bass'), spread over more than 3.4 million sq km (1.3 million sq mi) of Pacific Ocean.

MAUI, HAWAII, USA

PU'UPIHA CEMETERY

It looks like every other relaxing beach – except for the gravestones. Outside of the town of Lahaina on Maui's west coast, the 'Cemetery in the Sand' tells an intriguing story of Hawaiian history. In the late 1800s, large numbers of Chinese and Japanese immigrants flocked to Hawaii seeking work in the sugar industry. When they died, their bones were sent back home to Asia to be buried. But as the years passed, the Asian community began to bury their dead in Hawaii and chose this peaceful spot on the beach. One side of the cemetery is Chinese and the other is Japanese. Beyond the wharf is an ancient Hawaiian burial site, revealing that this has been a popular resting place for centuries.

LONGITUDE -180°/-120°

MAUI, HAWAII, USA

RAINBOW EUCALYPTUS TREES

A drive along Maui's iconic Road to Hana will take you past lush rainforests, secluded beaches and spectacular waterfalls. Venture deeper into the forest and you'll discover an extraordinary sight – a grove of rainbow eucalyptus trees. At first glance, you might think each trunk has been painstakingly painted by hand, but these masterpieces are entirely the work of nature. Each year, the trees shed their bark, revealing the brilliant young green bark below. As the bark ages, it turns vivid shades of red, orange, grey and purple. Because sections of bark shed at different times of the year, the trees become streaked with an ever-changing kaleidoscope of colour!

These unusual multi-coloured trees are one of Hawaii's many natural wonders.

LONGITUDE -120°/-60°

MAUI, HAWAII, USA
PAPAKŌLEA BEACH

Hawaiians call it Papakōlea because the kolea bird (golden plover) is a regular visitor, but to sightseers, it is known as the 'green-sand beach'. Found in a secluded cove, this spectacular natural wonder is one of only four green-sand beaches in the world. Its special colour comes from tiny grains of olivine – a type of semi-precious green rock usually only found deep underground. The rocks were made around 49,000 years ago when the nearby Mauna Loa volcano erupted, then broken down slowly over the years by the wind and rain.

LONGITUDE -60°/0°

According to local beliefs, taking sand from here will result in a curse from Pele, the Hawaiian goddess of fire. If that doesn't stop you, note that it's also illegal and you can be fined up to $100,000 – so be sure to shake out your sandals!

EKLUTNA, ALASKA, USA
SPIRIT HOUSES

In the graveyard of St Nicholas Orthodox Church in the Indigenouns village of Eklutna, Alaska, is a mini city of colourful 'spirit houses'. Built by the local Dena'ina Athabascan people, these tiny dwellings reflect the blending of beliefs between the Dena'ina and the Russian Orthodox Church.

Traditionally, the Dena'ina used to cremate their dead and place the ashes in birch-bark baskets in a tree or by a riverbank, leaving the spirit free to journey to the next life. When Russian Orthodox missionaries and fur traders arrived here in the early 1800s, they introduced their own beliefs – that the dead should be buried, not cremated. As the two cultures mixed, a new tradition began.

When a family member dies, they are buried in the cemetery of the church and a blanket is laid over their grave to provide warmth and comfort. A 'spirit home' is then placed on top, along with farewell gifts, giving the deceased souls somewhere safe to stay as they wait to pass from this world to the next. Over the years, many of the houses have been left to crumble, in keeping with the Athabascan belief that the dead should be allowed to return to the Earth.

Each spirit house is painted in the family's traditional colours. Most also feature the Russian Orthodox three-barred cross.

BRITISH COLUMBIA, CANADA

THE FELLED GOLDEN SPRUCE

Among a sea of green in the Haida Gwaii forest, a bright yellow spruce tree stood out like a single sunflower in a meadow. Its golden colour was caused by a genetic mutation that deprived the tree of the chlorophyll (green pigment) usually found in trees. The tree, pictured right, was 50m (164ft) high and played an important role in the legends of the Indigenous Haida people. That is, until 1997, when an environmental activist cut it down ... to protest cutting down trees! You can hike the Golden Spruce Trail to visit the trunk of the once mighty tree on the riverbank. Despite its fall, the tree lives on. Cuttings were taken from it and spread all across British Columbia. Someday the little sprucelings will be as tall and golden as their mum once was.

LONGITUDE -180°/-120°

This image shows how the tree used to look before it was felled in the mid-1990s.

CALIFORNIA, USA

CALIFORNIA'S LOST COAST

There are still places here that remain untouched. Up in northern California, Route 1 turns inland to avoid coastline that's too rugged for a highway. If you're not scared off by the unpaved logging roads, keep along the water – and you'll discover the Lost Coast.

From spectacular cliffs to windswept beaches, the Lost Coast is a 100km (62mi) stretch of California that is virtually off the radar because it's so hard to get to. But if you put in the work, you might find yourself camping in an abandoned settler's cabin and gazing up at old-growth redwood trees.

Don't be alarmed if a herd of elk graze past you as you hike across lonely but mesmerising landscapes, from the Sinkyone Wilderness State Park to the King Range National Conservation Area. This is a place worth preserving, to keep it a hidden wonder for generations to come.

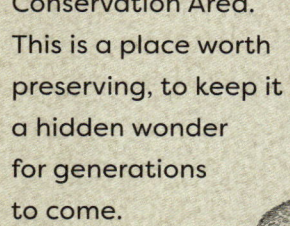

LONGITUDE -180°/-120°

CALIFORNIA, USA
MAMMOTH RUBBING ROCKS

Have you ever wondered how massive animals like mammoths scratched their backs? The discovery of a series of large boulders on the coast of north California may just hold the answer. When scientists examined the rocks, they discovered they had unusually smooth, shiny surfaces around 3–4m (10–14ft) above the ground. At first, it was thought the surface may have been worn away over the years by the movement of glaciers. But tiny scratch marks inspired a new theory: that during the last ice age, around 15,000 to 30,000 years ago, the stones were used as scratching posts for passing mammoths.

We know that modern-day elephants and bison rub against tree trunks or rocks to rid themselves of mud or parasites and relieve itching. It's thought that mammoths did the same on these enormous boulders (the shiny patches are about shoulder height for a mammoth!). Over time, the repeated rubbing smoothed the rocks leaving the shiny, polished surfaces we see today. As well as being handy scratching posts, the stones may also have helped shelter the mammoths from the wind.

LONGITUDE -180°/-120°

BRITISH COLUMBIA, CANADA
WHISTLER TRAIN WRECK SITE

LONGITUDE -180°/-120°

Street art in the middle of the forest? That's what was created when some local graffiti artists started spraying their work across abandoned train carriages in a forest outside the city. It all started in 1956, when a train was travelling too fast through the canyon and derailed. A logging company cleared the railroad by dragging the wrecked train cars into the woods, where they were left to rust.

Over the years, local artists have transformed the place into a colourful art installation. A suspension bridge crosses the Cheakamus River, leading you to the arty wreck site. But it's not just for artists! Mountain bikers have also made use of the site, building jumps and rails around the trains to create a woodsy bike playground.

THE WAVE ORGAN

SAN FRANCISCO, CALIFORNIA, USA

With this interactive piece of art, you don't just see the bay, you hear the bay. Standing on a small jetty, you can take in views of the Golden Gate Bridge and the infamous Alcatraz Island prison. Keep your ears open and you can hear the 25 organ pipes that artist Peter Richards installed at various levels around the jetty. As the water rushes in and out of the pipes, notes come out! Stand on this masterpiece with the wind in your hair and listen to the sea sing you its song.

LONGITUDE -180°/-120°

TUALATIN, OREGON, USA
THE GIANT PUMPKIN REGATTA

Every October, people gather for the West Coast Giant Pumpkin Regatta – where competitors carve out the centre of a giant pumpkin (and we do mean giant), get inside, and race across the lake. Pumpkins aren't particularly seaworthy, which is half the fun! The sight of them bobbing and bouncing in the water is what makes this race so special. The fastest pumpkin (and the paddler who manages to stay inside it) wins!

LONGITUDE -180°/-120°

SAN JOSE, CALIFORNIA, USA

WINCHESTER MYSTERY HOUSE

When her husband died, Sarah Winchester inherited the family fortune – made off of the invention of the Winchester rifle. That money came at a price, though. The legend goes that Sarah believed she was being haunted by the spirits of people who had been shot and killed by Winchester rifles. When a psychic told her that she needed to outwit the spirits in order to survive, Sarah got to work. She bought an unfinished farmhouse in San Jose, California, and had workmen renovating the house 24 hours a day for 38 years. Staircases lead to nowhere, doors open onto brick walls, and sometimes the only way into a room is through a cabinet. Always trying to stay one step ahead of the ghosts, Sarah slept in a different room every night – there are 160 of them in the house! It is said that she often wore a veil and held nightly séances. Sarah died peacefully in her sleep, at age 82. Her house was auctioned off to the highest bidder, who turned it into a tourist attraction.

LONGITUDE -180°/-120°

Fly above a spider
the size of a skyscraper p57

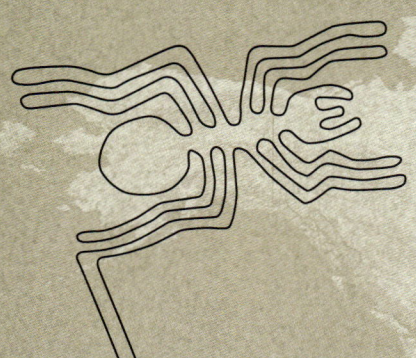

Get up close
to polar bears p40

LONGITUDE
-120°/-60°

Waddle with penguins
on a steaming
black-sand beach p73

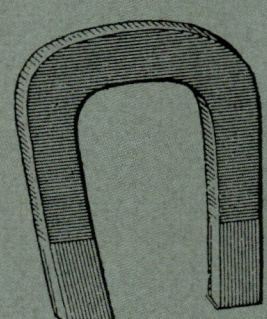

Drive tanks
and crush cars p46

Feel the force
of a mysterious
Easter Island rock p36

Kick off your shoes
and throw them into
a tree p32

Paddle alongside
little piggies p54

Sort the junk
from the treasures in a
classic-car graveyard p44

OSOYOOS, BRITISH COLUMBIA, CANADA
SPOTTED LAKE

For most of the year, this otherworldly lake looks like any other. But during the hot summer months, as the sun beats down on the baking desert landscape, it undergoes an amazing transformation. Much of the water evaporates, leaving behind shimmering spotted pools, which can be blue, green or yellow depending on the mix of minerals contained within them.

For the Syilx people of the Okanagan Nation, each of the lake's different circles holds its own special medicinal and healing properties. For centuries, they have come to the lake to perform ceremonies and treat various ailments. As this is sacred land, visitors are not allowed to visit the lake itself, but you can catch a glimpse of the pools from a lookout point along Highway 3.

LONGITUDE -120°/-60°

Researchers say the conditions at Osoyoos Spotted Lake are what the landscape would have been like on ancient Mars!

NEVADA, USA
FLY RANCH GEYSER

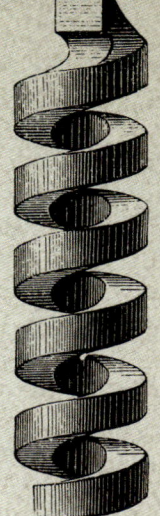

Unlike geysers that form naturally over millions of years, the spectacular Fly Ranch Geyser in Nevada's Black Rock Desert is an accidental human creation. In the 1960s, engineers drilled into the ground, attempting to tap into the geothermal energy source below. The project was abandoned, but the engineers failed to properly seal the well. Over the years, hot, mineral-rich water streamed out, forming rocky cones on top of a massive mound, surrounded by terraces and shallow pools. The brilliant hues of green and red come from the multi-coloured algae that thrive on the geyser's terraces.

Fly Ranch is on private property so you can't just 'rock up' – you will need to book a private tour to get up close to this accidental watery wonderland.

LONGITUDE -120°/-60°

This rainbow-coloured marvel spews nearly boiling hot water 1.5m (5ft) into the air!

HIGHWAY 50, NEVADA, USA
THE SHOE TREE

LONGITUDE -120°/-60°

Called the Loneliest Road, Highway 50 stretches for miles through empty desert – until you get to the Shoe Tree! Legend has it that a newlywed couple got into a fight beneath the tree. The bride threatened to walk home and the groom tossed her shoes into the tree to prevent her from leaving! They made up, and a tradition was born. People threw their shoes up into the tree for years, until the original tree was cut down in 2010. Now a nearby cottonwood named Shoe Tree Junior does the job. If you find yourself travelling down the Loneliest Road, be sure to bring an old pair of shoes to add to the story.

DEATH VALLEY NATIONAL PARK, CALIFORNIA, USA
RACETRACK PLAYA

You don't get the name 'Death Valley' without some serious street cred. Situated in the northern part of Death Valley National Park is an unpaved danger zone called Racetrack Road that cuts through 43km (27mi) of vast desert. It leads to the Racetrack Playa, a huge dry lake bed dotted with boulders. But these aren't just any ordinary boulders. These rocks, some as heavy as 318kg (700lb), can move, leaving tracks in the dirt! How, you ask? The movement of the rocks was a mystery until 2014 when scientists finally solved it.

It has to do with the extreme temperatures of the area. In the winter, a thin layer of ice covers the playa. On sunny days, the ice cracks and winds rush down from the mountains, pushing the ice sheets apart. When the ice completely melts, the boulders are left in their new positions. Even though we now know the secret of this place, that doesn't take away from its stark beauty.

LONGITUDE -120°/-60°

BLYTHE, CALIFORNIA, USA

BLYTHE GEOGLYPHS

You may have heard of the Nazca Lines in Peru (see page 57), but did you know that California has its own giant figures, etched into the sand of the Mojave Desert? Many mysteries still surround the Blythe Geoglyphs or 'Blythe Giants'. It's not clear who created the figures, or even when, but it's thought they were made somewhere between 450 and 2,000 years ago and were the handiwork of the Native Americans who lived along the Colorado River.

According to the local Mohave and Quechan people, the figures include Mastamho, the creator of all life, and Hatakulya, a mountain lion who helped in the Creation. Exactly why these ancient drawings were made and who for has been puzzling anthropologists for decades. However, seeing as they can only be viewed properly from the air, it's likely they were intended as a tribute or message to the heavens above.

LONGITUDE -120°/-60°

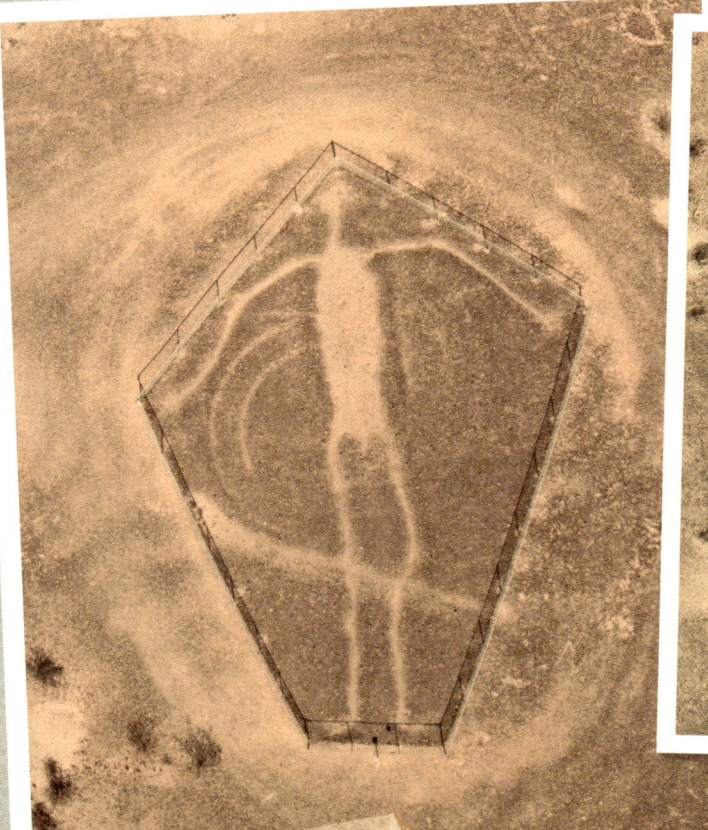

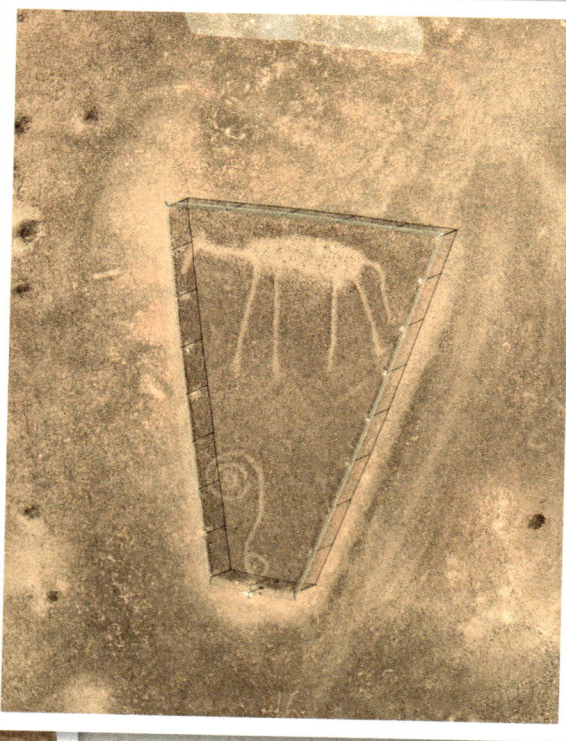

The figures were scratched into the earth by scraping away the dark rocks to reveal the lighter soil underneath. The largest of the carvings is (52m) 171ft long!

UTAH, USA
NINE MILE CANYON

Tucked away in the red sandstone mountains of the Utah wilderness sits one of the world's largest and most ancient art galleries. Running along the walls of this canyon – which is actually 74km (46mi) long – are more than 10,000 prehistoric petroglyphs and pictographs carved into or painted onto the rocks. Most were created by the native Fremont people, who lived here between 900 and 1250 CE, but some date back as far as 5000 BCE. In the 16th century, the Ute people arrived in the area and added their own distinctive artworks to this extraordinary gallery. The scenes tell a story of what life was like for the local peoples through the centuries, showing everything from hunting and farming to family life. You can also visit the pit homes of the Fremont, which kept them warm in the winter and cool in the summer.

LONGITUDE -120°/-60°

EASTER ISLAND, CHILE

THE NAVEL OF THE WORLD

LONGITUDE -120°/-60°

For such a tiny speck of land, Easter Island is crammed with an amazing number of archaeological sites. The most famous are the moai, giant human statues that are scattered all over the island like eerie guardians from another world. Yet one of the most fascinating things on Easter Island is a perfectly round stone surrounded by four smaller round stones. Legend has it that King Hotu Matu'a, the first settler of Easter Island in around 800 CE, brought the stone here to represent the 'navel of the world'. Meaning, if Earth was shaped like a body, this would be its belly button!

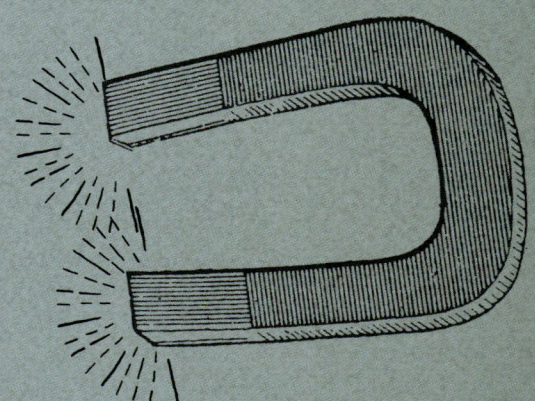

That's not the only curious thing about the stone: it's also magnetic. If you place your compass on the rock, it will lose its direction. The Rapa Nui people who lived here believed this to be the work of magical forces, although scientists will tell you it's because the rock contains magnetic elements within it.

MARIETA ISLANDS, MEXICO

HIDDEN BEACH

True to its name, Hidden Beach can't be seen from the outside and is only accessible through a long water tunnel that links it to the Pacific Ocean. If you were to swim or kayak through the tunnel, you'd arrive at a doughnut-hole-shaped beach made up of cream-coloured sand. The island's strange shape is rumoured to be the result of modern bomb testing by the Mexican government, though scientists have many theories.

This secluded beach can only be reached at low tide. As well as people, it is visited by sea turtles, dolphins and manta rays.

LONGITUDE -120°/-60°

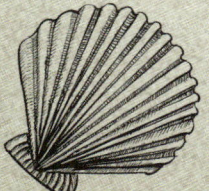
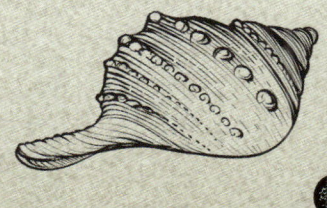

CHIHUAHUA, MEXICO

CAVE OF THE CRYSTALS

Almost 20 years ago, two brothers working at a mining company stumbled onto what seemed like the set of a science-fiction movie. Enormous, translucent crystals criss-crossed the interior of a cave nearly 304m (1,000ft) below the ground. The cave was once flooded with water, but when the mining company pumped it dry, the 500,000-year-old crystals were uncovered. They're the largest crystals found on the planet and made of the mineral selenite, which is so soft you can scratch it with your fingernail. After its discovery, researchers visited the cave wearing special suits to protect them from the blazing temperatures, which could reach up to 49°C (120°F). It was impossible to stay in the cave unprotected for more than a few minutes.

In 2017, mining operations ceased and water was released back into the cave, allowing the crystals to start growing again. But flooding it with water means no human can enter, and the crystals are currently lost to us once more.

CHURCHILL, MANITOBA, CANADA

THE POLAR BEAR CAPITAL OF THE WORLD

LONGITUDE -120°/-60°

Ever wondered what it would be like to come face to face with a polar bear? Find out by visiting Churchill, dubbed the 'Polar Bear Capital of the World'. This remote town on the edge of Hudson Bay lies on the migration route of polar bears making their way to their icy Arctic hunting grounds. In recent years, the bay has taken longer to freeze, forcing the bears to stay longer on land and even venture into the town itself to sniff out food. Residents are advised to have bear-proof bins, to always check outside before leaving a building, and to stay in well-lit areas. It's definitely not a good idea to go out alone after dark – these mighty carnivores can kill most animals with a swipe of their giant paw!

To see the bears safely, you can join a tour in a bear-proof buggy into the icy wilderness beyond the city limits. The buggies have a steel mesh floor, so you can see the bears up close as they wander underneath.

INDIAHOMA, OKLAHOMA, USA

WICHITA MOUNTAINS WILDLIFE REFUGE

Hundreds of years ago, vast herds of bison roamed the prairie grasslands of America's Great Plains. They were an important part of the landscape and the lives of the Native American people. By the late 1800s, after the mass slaughter of bison and the decimation of their habitat by European settlers, they were on the brink of extinction.

But in 1907, 15 American bison from New York Zoo boarded a train and journeyed across the country to the newly created Wichita Forest Reserve in Oklahoma. There, they were greeted by the Comanche chief Quanah Parker, who had helped persuade the US president to open the reserve. Today, a herd of 650 of these gentle giants can be seen grazing freely on the prairies once more.

LONGITUDE -120°/-60°

CAYO, BELIZE

ACTUN TUNICHIL MUKNAL

Journey around 1.6km (1mi) underground into this vast cavern full of history. A thousand years ago, the ancient Maya – an indigenous people of Mesoamerica (modern-day Mexico and Central America) – tried to find a route to the underworld through this cave. Inside are huge stalagmites and stalactites, along with broken pots that were once used to offer food – or blood – to the gods.

Even more unique and disturbing are the dozen or so skeletons believed to belong to ancient human sacrifices. Most eerie of all is the so-called Crystal Maiden. Once thought to be the skeleton of a woman, scientists now say the bones are those of a young man. This long-dead Maya has lain here so long his bones have completely calcified, giving them a sparkling, crystalline appearance.

LONGITUDE -120°/-60°

The glittering bones of the 'Crystal Maiden' or 'Crystal Prince' reveal just why the Maya might have chosen this mystical place as their channel to the gods.

WHITE, GEORGIA, USA

OLD CAR CITY

People sure love their cars... even the junkers. Over 4,000 of these beloved rust-mobiles languish here in Old Car City, and the forest has reclaimed many of them. It's one-part junkyard, one-part classic car museum and one-part nature preserve, with 9.65km (6mi) of nature trails winding through the area.

Among the vintage treasures here are numerous cars, trucks, vans and even a couple of school buses.

ZARCERO, COSTA RICA
PARQUE FRANCISCO ALVARADO

Take a stroll in this lovely park in Costa Rica and you'll notice something unusual about the topiaries. Stretching out from a 17th-century church, the park is filled with surreal shapes and figures. In the 1960s, the gardener Evangelisto Blanco decided to let his imagination run wild. He shaped the hedges into melting archways, friendly dinosaurs and otherworldly creatures. The garden continues to delight visitors to this day.

LONGITUDE -180°/-120°

MORGANTAN, GEORGIA, USA

TANK TOWN USA

Tank Town USA's motto is 'Drive Tanks. Crush Cars'. That pretty much sums it up. Here, visitors can drive tanks... over cars! You can also take a spin on a 18-tonne (20-ton) construction excavator and dig some holes. If you're obsessed with tanks, this place is a dream!

LONGITUDE -120°/-60°

A military tank crushes a blue car.

DIQUÍS DELTA, COSTA RICA

DIQUÍS SPHERES

LONGITUDE -120°/-60°

These perfectly formed stone spheres are a mysterious reminder of the Diquís civilisation that existed in Costa Rica from around 700 BCE to 1530 CE. The stones were found in 1939 by workers clearing the jungles of the Diquís Delta to make way for banana plantations. There were rumours that gold was hidden inside them, so workers drilled holes into them and even blew

There are around 300 Diquís spheres. Some are small enough to hold in your hand, others are over 2m (6ft) in diameter.

some up with dynamite! What the stones were really used for, no one knows. But the way that some of them are aligned suggests they may have been solar calendars. Or they may have been used to show off power: the bigger the rock, the stronger the chief!

HAVANA, CUBA

FUSTERLANDIA

In the 1990s, Cuban artist José Fuster decided to spruce up his house. But his DIY project soon extended beyond his own home, eventually covering several city blocks, including his neighbours' houses, offices, bus stops and benches. Nicknamed Fusterlandia, this ever-growing work of art features fanciful mosaic tile creations and sculptures in every colour of the rainbow.

There's a Cuban theme to the sprawling artwork. Inside a huge mural painting of the Granma yacht, you can spot important historical figures Fidel Castro, Che Guevara and Camilo Cienfuegos. Reproductions of the Cuban flag are everywhere. A line of houses have the words 'Viva Cuba' emblazoned on their chimneys.

The brightest spot in the whole 'hood is Fuster's own house. Murals cover every surface. There are sculpted arches and swirling ceramic trees too! In the centre of it all, there is a pool painted like an undersea fantasy with mermaids, fishermen and a giant octopus.

The art is a celebration of daily Cuban life, folk stories and important historical figures, and was intended to create a sense of pride among residents.

LONGITUDE -120°/-60°

GRAND CAYMAN, CAYMAN ISLANDS

HELL

Journey to Hell and back – literally. Tucked away on the heavenly island of Grand Cayman is a place called Hell, which contains a group of ancient limestone formations. These spiky black rocks definitely look like they've risen up out of the underworld. Although the barren landscape is at odds with the rest of this tropical paradise, the locals embrace it. The post office and gift shop welcome you with a bright red 'Welcome to Hell' sign, and you can meet 'Satan' here. (Okay, it's actually a guy named Ivan Farrington, but it's still pretty hellish around here!)

NEAR MIAMI, FLORIDA, USA
CORAL CASTLE

LONGITUDE -120°/-60°

This massive sculpture garden in Florida is as mysterious as it is astounding. It was a labour of love for Latvian immigrant Edward Leedskalnin, who created these sculptures after being rejected by his promised bride. He made them entirely by hand out of coral stone local to Florida. But how he did it remains a mystery – he worked at night by lantern light so no one could watch him. While Leedskalnin came from a family of stonemasons in Latvia, modern scholars still don't know how he built this immense park on his own since many of the sculptures are carved out of a single piece of stone, and some of them reach over 8m (25ft) tall. Just how did one man wield such massive rocks?

TUNGURAHUA PROVINCE, ECUADOR

THE SWING AT THE END OF THE WORLD

Way up high in the Ecuadorian jungle is the world's most perilous treehouse. Perched on the edge of a canyon, the Casa del Arbol is actually a seismic observation station. It's there to keep an eye on its next-door neighbour Tungurahua, an active volcano. But the best part of the treehouse is its swing. Hanging from a branch, it's just a little plank of wood suspended by two ropes. And unlike the swings at your local playground, there's no harness, net or any safety features at all. People who do brave the swing, though, are rewarded with an incredible view of the canyon.

LONGITUDE -120°/-60°

LIMA, PERU
MUSEO DEL CEREBRO

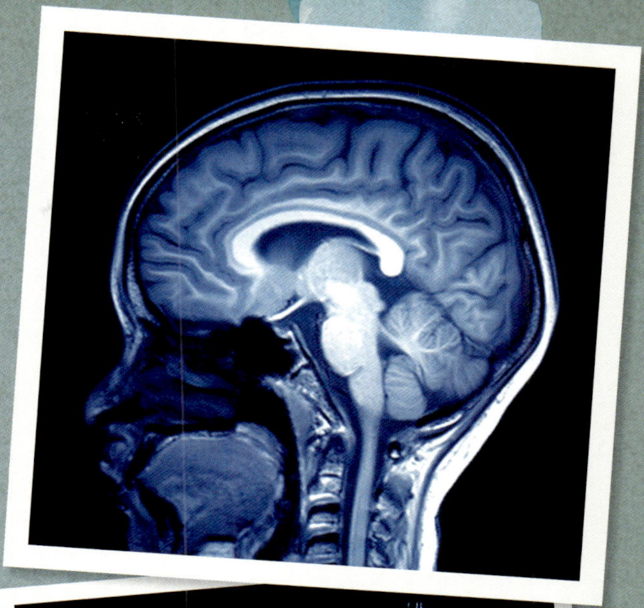

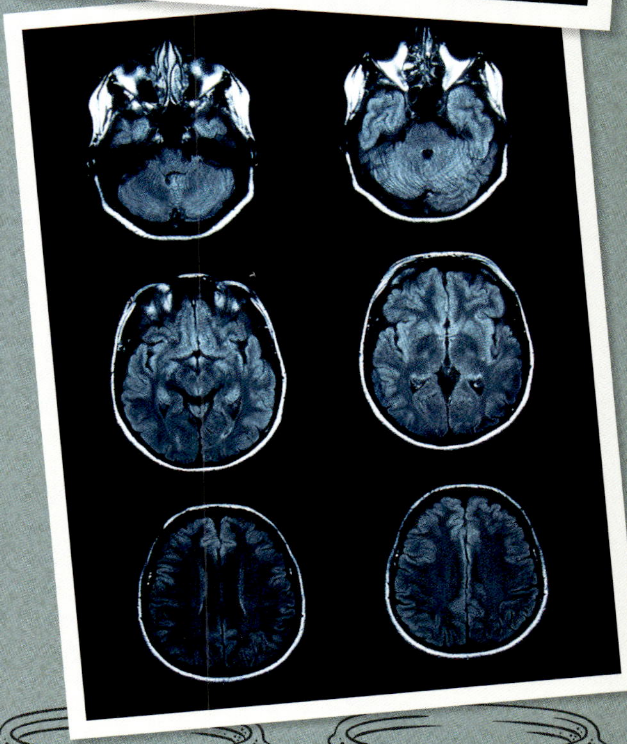

This museum in Lima is a zombie's heaven. In a plain building behind the Institute of Neurological Science is a collection of more than 3,000 brains. They're all contained in neatly labelled and formaldehyde-filled jars. Each brain displays the damage caused by various diseases. Diana Rivas is a neuropathologist, someone who studies diseases of the nervous system, and heads the museum. She also performs autopsies here, collecting new specimens to put on display. While most visitors are medical students, anyone who wants to learn more about the most interesting organ in our bodies can visit.

This lesser-known museum is one of only a few places in the world where you can get a glimpse at what's going on inside our brains.

LONGITUDE -120°/-60°

BIG MAJOR CAY, THE BAHAMAS

PIG BEACH

You've heard the expression 'happy as a pig in mud' but what about 'happy as a pig in seawater'? On the uninhabited island of Big Major Cay in the Bahamas, that's just what you'll find – a bunch of cute piggy paddlers.

No one knows how the pigs got here in the first place. Were they survivors of a shipwreck carrying livestock to Nassau, the country's capital, about 140km (90mi) away? Did some seafaring explorer bring the pigs here? However they arrived, these pigs are wild but friendly and love the ocean more than any muddy farm.

Visitors can swim alongside the pigs in the crystal clear waters.

ANTIOQUIA, COLOMBIA
LA CUEVA DEL ESPLENDOR

What's the best thing to do after a long hike? If you answered 'jump in a pool', you'll love the Cave of Splendour near the small town of Jardín in Colombia. First, you can follow a hiking or horseback-riding route through lush green mountains which comes to a steep riverbed trail.

The reward for all that exercise? A glistening waterfall tumbling through the roof of a glorious cave, sculpted by the rushing water over hundreds of years. The deep, refreshing water at the base of the waterfall is the perfect place to take a plunge and cool off.

LONGITUDE -120°/-60°

EL PENÕN DE GUATAPÉ

ANTIOQUIA, COLOMBIA

LONGITUDE -120°/-60°

This giant stone rises 200m (650ft) into the air over the surrounding landscape. It's so awe-inspiring that the Indigenous Tahamies people worshipped it centuries ago. But it wasn't until 1954 that someone actually made it to the top of the rock. A group of friends wedged boards into the single crack running down the length of the stone. It took them five days, but they finally made it all the way to the summit. Now visitors can follow in their footsteps, using a stone staircase that's been built into the same crack. Once at the top, hikers are rewarded with stunning views from the lookout tower of the nearby lakes and islands.

NAZCA DESERT, PERU

NAZCA LINES

Take a flight above the Nazca Desert in Peru and you'll see more than sand and rock. High above the ground, animals carved into the earth will take shape beneath you: a monkey with a curved tail, a hummingbird with a long, thin beak and a spider the size of a skyscraper.

The lines and shapes scattered over this 803 sq km (310 sq mi) stretch of the Nazca Plain remain an archaeological mystery. It's believed they were created by the ancient Nazca people who lived here from 200 BCE to 500 CE. They were made by removing earth and rocks from the desert, exposing the light-coloured sand beneath.

The designs have stayed intact for so long due to the climate – particularly the lack of rain, wind or erosion.

But because the huge etchings can't be seen from the ground, it wasn't until the dawn of air travel in the 1930s that pilots began to spot them from the sky. How did the Nazca people create these perfect designs without being able to see them fully? And why were they created in the first place? One theory is that shapes were intended as messages to the gods asking them for water in this very dry place.

LONGITUDE -120°/-60°

ZIPAQUIRÁ, COLOMBIA
CATEDRAL DE SAL

Cathedrals are made out of brick and stone, right? Think again! This Colombian cathedral was carved by removing 228,000 tonnes (250,000 tons) of salt and is one of only three salt cathedrals in the world. Descend over 183m (600ft) below ground into a salt mine and you'll find yourself inside a stunning sanctuary.

Intricate Catholic symbolis fill the 14 chapels that make up the church. Dramatic lighting adds to the moody atmosphere, especially in the central nave. There, a mammoth cross shines from top to bottom, casting a truly heavenly glow.

LONGITUDE -180°/-120°

SLEEPY HOLLOW, NEW YORK, USA

SLEEPY HOLLOW CEMETERY

You may have read *The Legend of Sleepy Hollow* about a headless horseman that roams the tiny town of Sleepy Hollow in search of his head. But did you know that Sleepy Hollow is a real place? North of New York City, USA, lies an idyllic stretch of the Hudson Valley. There you'll find Sleepy Hollow Cemetery, with its rows of weathered gravestones sunk into the ground.

Some plots contain famous names in American history: Rockefeller, Carnegie, and the author of *The Legend of Sleepy Hollow* himself, Washington Irving, are all buried here. There's no denying its gloomy, atmospheric appeal, but you wouldn't want to linger too long after midnight here, or you may find yourself running from the headless horseman who made this place famous.

In the story, the headless horseman (above right) was a soldier who lost his head in the American Revolutionary War after being shot by a canon.

LONGITUDE -180°/-120°

PATAGONIA, CHILE

CUEVA DEL MILODÓN NATURAL MONUMENT

LONGITUDE -180°/-120°

Catch a glimpse of what life was like more than 10,000 years ago in these remote caves in Chile's Patagonia region. Getting here is half the adventure, whether you take a bumpy flight, a very long bus ride, or a boat through stunning fjords. Once you arrive, you'll be greeted by a life-sized replica of a giant ground sloth (*Mylodon*). Remains of this long-extinct animal were found here, alongside the bones of other prehistoric animals, such as the sabre-toothed cat *Smilodon*. Stone tools and human remains show that people also lived in the area as early as 6000 BCE.

This skull shows the fearsome fangs of a *Smilodon*, which prowled the area between around 2.5 million to 8,200 years ago.

MARAS, PERU
MORAY

The Inca were known for their masterful engineering and this amphitheatre is no exception. In a remote part of the Sacred Valley, grass-covered terraces are carved into the landscape – designed and positioned in relation to the Sun and wind. There's actually a difference in temperature from the top of the bowl to the bottom, meaning the climate on each terrace varies slightly. In fact, each terrace corresponds to different growing conditions across what was the Inca Empire. It's likely they used the terraces to test different crops, studying which climate was best suited to grow potato, maize or quinoa. Talk about amazing technology!

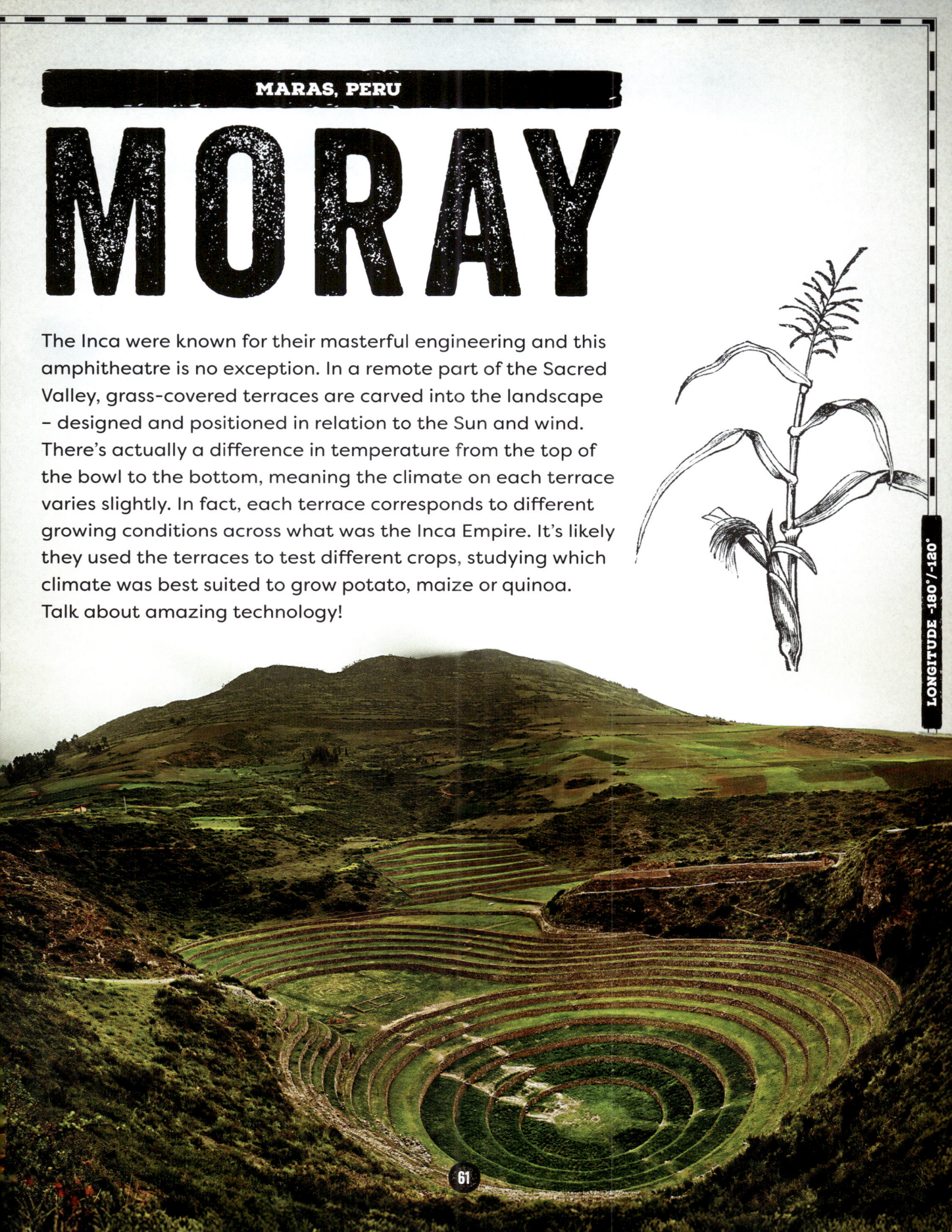

LONGITUDE -180°/-120°

CHILOÉ, CHILE

DOCK OF SOULS

The Dock of Souls looks like a dock to nowhere. Located on the island of Chiloé in southern Chile, the wooden pier curves towards the edge of a cliff and ends abruptly with a drop to the sea. It looks like a mistake, but it's actually a sculpture by Chilean artist Marcelo Orellana Rivera. He was inspired by the Indigenous Mapuche people's legend of Tempilcahue. According to the myth, Tempilcahue ferried the souls of the dead across the water to the afterlife. Sit on the edge of the Dock of Souls at sunset and you can just imagine Tempilcahue pulling up to the dock in his ferry, ready to take waiting souls to the beyond.

LONGITUDE -120˚/-60˚

CANAS, PERU

Q'ESWACHAKA ROPE BRIDGE

When the Inca lived here 600 years ago, they used rope bridges to cross canyons and rivers. Now the Q'eswachaka Bridge is the last one left. It's made out of ichu (a type of grass) and hangs high above the Apurímac River. But don't fear, the bridge is remade every June by the local Quechua communities.

LONGITUDE -120°/-60°

The bridge ropes are woven by the women of the communities, then collected at a yearly festival and braided together by the *chakarauwaq* (engineers). The old bridge is dropped into the river and replaced by the new one – then a ceremony takes place to thank the mountain spirits for the continued safety of anyone who crosses this wondrous bridge.

LA PAZ, BOLIVIA

WITCHES' MARKET

La Paz is a modern city, but there is still a deep belief in the old ways here. One of the best ways to experience the fascinating Aymara folk medicine tradition, which has been practised in Bolivia for over a thousand years, is at the Witches' Market. The market is frequented by *brujas* (witches) and *kallawaya* doctors (medicine men), who offer to read fortunes and heal the sick with prayers, herbs and potions.

One of their more surprising tools is the guinea pig. These adorable rodents identify the patient's ailment. From there a treatment is carried out, ranging from laying hands on a broken bone to passing an egg over an infected part of the body, all while chanting and praying.

Stalls are stacked with items such as medicinal plants, dried frogs and snakes, owl feathers, and amulets to attract good fortune and protect against evil spirits.

LONGITUDE -120°/-60°

UYUNI, BOLIVIA

CEMENTERIO DE TRENES

High up on the Andean plateau in Bolivia there lies a train graveyard. During the 19th century, the town of Uyuni was a major transportation hub for mining companies. British railway lines were built to connect the town to ports in the Pacific Ocean, and trains ran back and forth from the mines to the ports. But by the mid-20th century, mining there was no longer profitable and Britain wasn't particularly welcome in the area. The trains were no use anymore, so were abandoned and left here to rust.

LONGITUDE -120°/-60°

These rusty trains are a reminder of Bolivia's golden age of silver and tin mining – and fun to climb on!

CULEBRA, PUERTO RICO (USA)

TANKS OF FLAMENCO BEACH

On this beautiful stretch of beach, two decommissioned tanks sit still in the sand. Although Flamenco Beach is now a perfectly laid-back place to soak up some sun, back in the late 1930s, the US Navy decided it was the perfect place to prepare for war. Bombing practice and military exercises took place here for decades and got more intense during the Vietnam War.

By 1971, the Culebra locals had had enough – their protests led to the US Navy ceasing all military activity on the beach.

The two tanks are all that remain of the military's presence. Puerto Ricans have covered them with graffiti art;, and today, they remain a colourful symbol of the power of resistance.

LONGITUDE -120°/-60°

SUCRE, BOLIVIA

PARQUE CRETÁCICO

LONGITUDE -120°/-60°

Get ready to cast your mind way, way back. Once upon a time, more than 66 million years ago, dinosaurs roamed the Earth here in Sucre, Bolivia. As they plodded or scurried across the muddy shores of the shallow lake, they left behind their footprints. Over time, these tracks were buried under layer upon layer of sediment which hardened to stone. Millions of years later, tectonic forces pushed the once-flat lakebed upwards to an almost vertical position, creating the Cal Orck'o wall.

Today, you'll find over 5,000 footprints seemingly travelling directly up the cliff, including those of armoured ankylosaurs, carnivorous theropods and long-necked sauropods. Home to the world's largest collection of dinosaur prints, this the perfect place to marvel at relics from a land before time.

VIRGIN ISLANDS (USA)
TEKTITE UNDERWATER HABITAT

It's a plot straight out of a science-fiction movie: a group of 'aquanauts' living in a bunker underwater, studying the effects of living in an extreme environment, and reporting the results to the government. But in 1969, this actually happened. The US government installed two metal cylinders at the bottom of the ocean off the island of St John in the Caribbean. Then they gathered four scientists who lived in the cylinders for 60 days. The crew breathed 92% nitrogen and 8% oxygen for the length of their mission (in comparison, we breathe 78% nitrogen and 21% oxygen in our air every day). At the end of the mission, they spent 19 hours in a decompression tank beforen surfacing, with the mission being declared a success.

The next year, an all-female crew took control of the facility for a series of shorter missions that were partially paid for by NASA. The research was intended to help train astronauts for space. It was these women who paved the way for female astronauts to be included on future US space missions.

The US government removed the actual habitat from the ocean decades ago, but if you strap on a snorkel mask and dive into the bay, you can still see the foundation pads in the seabed.

MONTSERRAT (UK)
SOUFRIÈRE HILLS VOLCANO

Life was peaceful on the small island of Montserrat, a British territory in the Caribbean. But on 18 July 1995, the Soufrière Hills volcano erupted and red-hot lava flowed across the island. The capital, Plymouth, was buried, as were many other towns and forests. Most of the island was left covered in ash. Two years later, the volcano erupted again, destroying even more of the island. As a result, most of the residents left, but those who stayed found a way to use the volcanic ruin to their advantage. This island, frozen in ash, is now a tourist destination. Visitors can see rooftops and church steeples peek out from under solidified ash in Plymouth, or visit the Montserrat Volcano Observatory to learn about the volcano's lively past... and take a guess when the still-active Soufrière Hills will erupt again.

LONGITUDE -120°/-60°

BEQUIA, ST VINCENT & THE GRENADINES
THE MOONHOLE

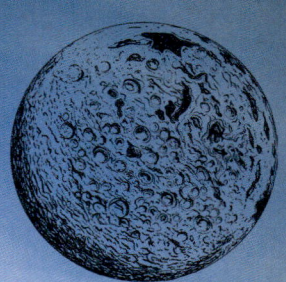

In the 1950s, Tom and Gladdi Johnston moved to Bequia and became fascinated by a local oddity called the Moonhole. A large natural rock archway, the Moonhole got its name because when the angle is just right, the archway frames the Moon. The Johnstons spent so much time camping there that they decided to build a house in that very spot. They didn't have any experience of building a house, but that didn't stop them. Their dream home flowed in and out of nature.

The floors were uneven, the walls constructed from rock, and everything else made of found objects like whalebone. Because it was so remote, the house didn't have running water; rainwater from the roofs was instead collected in cisterns. Today, the original house is uninhabitable, with dangerous rocks falling in on its roof, but you can still view the beautiful wreck from the sea.

ANTARCTICA
DECEPTION ISLAND

This active volcano in the remote South Shetland Islands is hiding more than a few secrets. Following a huge eruption 10,000 years ago, the volcano's crater collapsed and flooded with water, forming an incredible natural harbour. To get there, you must sail through a narrow break in the volcano's walls. This passageway has been known by a few names: Neptune's Bellows (because of the strong winds that blow through it), Dragon's Mouth and Hell's Gates. Not exactly a cheerful welcome!

Once you're in, you'll find a horseshoe-shaped bay with steaming black-sand beaches dotted with a colony of more than 100,000 breeding pairs of chinstrap penguins.

LONGITUDE -120°/-60°

Customise your own hand-crafted coffin p97

LONGITUDE -60°/0°

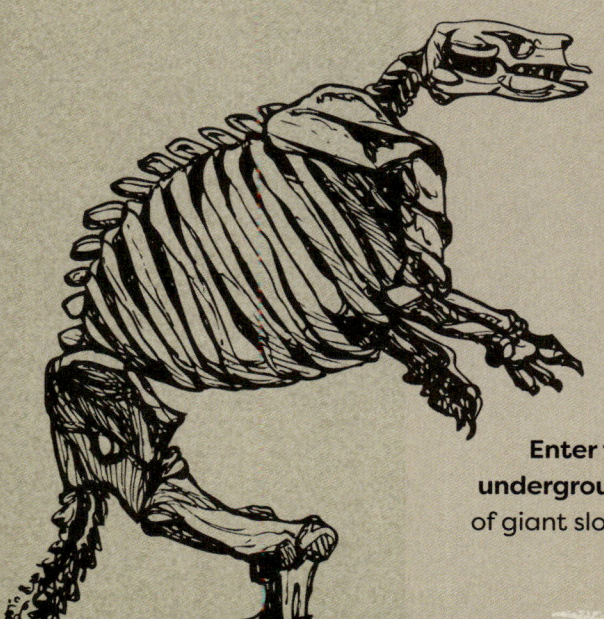

Enter the underground lair of giant sloths p76

Discover the wonders of pigeon poo at an ancient tannery p88

Step back in time at a prehistoric art gallery p82

Watch a frenzy of fishing at a sacred lake p96

BONITO, BRAZIL
GRUTA DO LAGO AZUL

Beneath a ceiling dripping with stalactites, a pool of crystalline turquoise water has gathered in this gorgeous grotto. Gruta do Lago Azul (Blue Lake Cave) is one of the largest flooded cavities on the planet and more than 70m (230ft) deep. In 1992, a diving team explored those vast depths. There they discovered...

LONGITUDE -60˚/0˚

...a treasure trove of prehistoric animal remains littering the grotto's floor, including the bones of giant sloths, which could be 3–4m (10–13ft) long.

ISLAND'S BAY, NEWFOUNDLAND AND LABRADOR, CANADA
L'ANSE AUX MEADOWS

In the 1960s, archaeologists investigating some grassy mounds on the windswept coast of Newfoundland made an incredible discovery. Buried beneath the ground were the remains of a Viking settlement dating from 990 to 1050 CE. This was proof, finally, that the first Europeans to set foot on North American soil were the Vikings – centuries before Christopher Columbus. These were not the original inhabitants of the area, though. Indigenous peoples lived here thousands of years before the Vikings.

Today, you can step back in time and imagine what life was like in the settlement. The site contains the remains of the camp, as well as a recreation of a Viking village, where you can try your hand at blacksmithing, weaving and axe throwing, or gather around the kitchen fire and hear tales of Eric the Red, Thor and other heroic figures from Viking tales. You can also climb aboard a replica Viking ship.

LONGITUDE -60°/0°

Viking homes were made with timber frames and thick blocks of dried peat. The roofs were covered with sod (grass and soil).

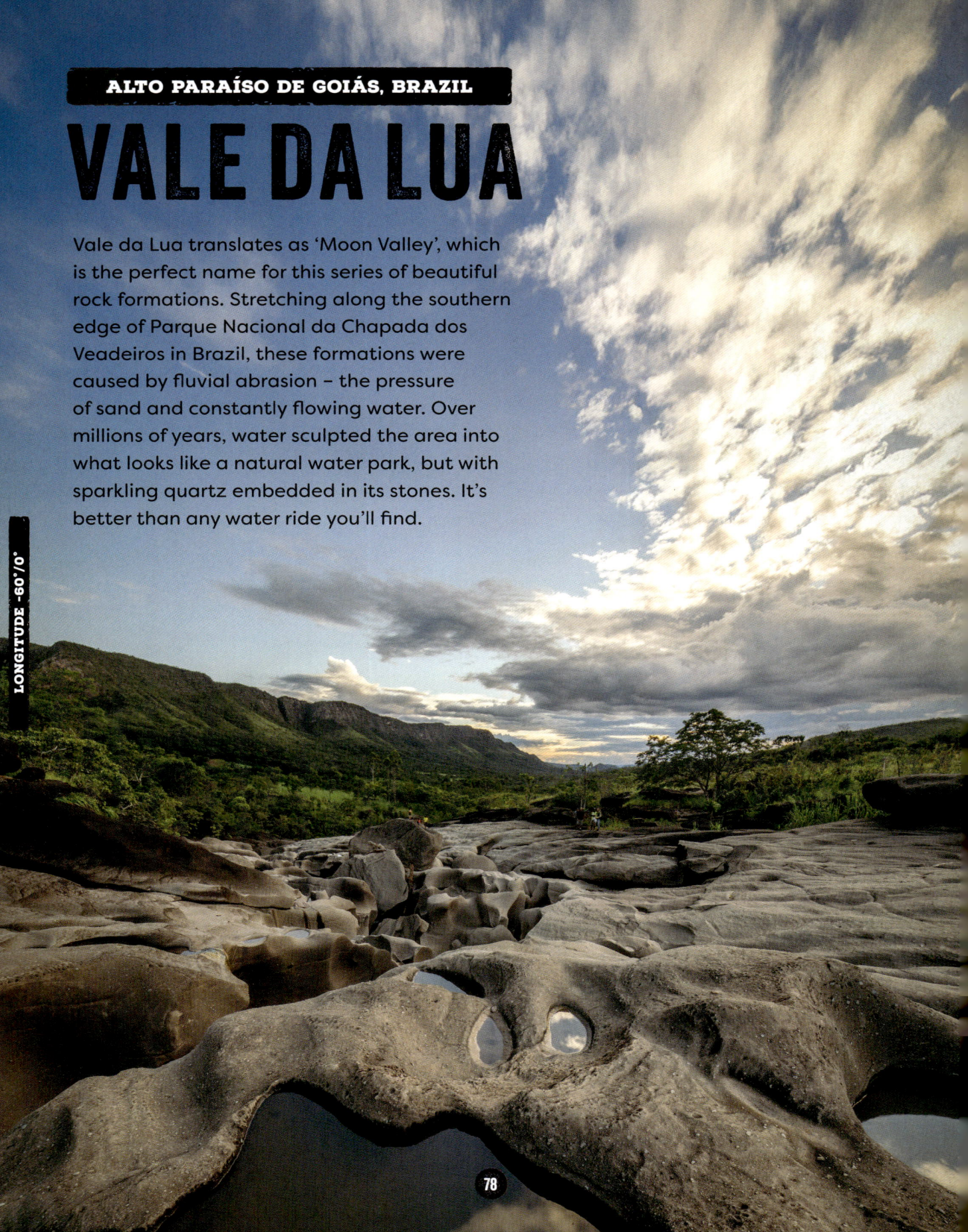

ALTO PARAÍSO DE GOIÁS, BRAZIL
VALE DA LUA

Vale da Lua translates as 'Moon Valley', which is the perfect name for this series of beautiful rock formations. Stretching along the southern edge of Parque Nacional da Chapada dos Veadeiros in Brazil, these formations were caused by fluvial abrasion – the pressure of sand and constantly flowing water. Over millions of years, water sculpted the area into what looks like a natural water park, but with sparkling quartz embedded in its stones. It's better than any water ride you'll find.

LONGITUDE -60°/0°

ILHA DA QUEIMADA GRANDE, BRAZIL
SNAKE ISLAND

If you hate snakes, this place is the stuff of nightmares. Ilha da Queimada Grande, off the coast of Brazil, is only small, but it's home to several thousand golden lancehead pit vipers. And these aren't just any snake – they can grow to over 1m (3ft) long and their venom is so powerful it can melt human flesh!

It wasn't always this way. The island used to be attached to the mainland, but rising sea levels cut it off, stranding the snakes on their island habitat. Left alone, the snakes survived on a diet of birds and were able to multiply fast, developing lethal venom. It may be the most dangerous island on the planet but never fear: the island is off-limits to everyone except researchers and the military.

LONGITUDE -60˚/0˚

MARANHÃO, BRAZIL

PARQUE NACIONAL DOS LENÇÓIS MARANHENSES

LONGITUDE -60°/0°

Are you dreaming? You'll think so seeing these mirage-like lagoons in the midst of towering sand dunes. Parque Nacional dos Lençóis Maranhenses in Brazil is a 1,548 sq km (598 sq mi) national treasure. With their crystal blue water shimmering against the bright white dunes, the lagoons seem to transcend reality. But dipping a toe into these refreshing pools of water would make anyone happy to be wide awake in this paradise.

PIAUÍ, BRAZIL

ROCK PAINTINGS OF PARQUE NACIONAL SERRA DA CAPIVARA

LONGITUDE -60°/0°

The red stone arches and bursts of greenery are remarkable enough at this national park and Unesco World Heritage site in Brazil. But take a stroll along the wooden walkways, and you'll see what's really special about this place. Some 40,000 prehistoric rock paintings decorate the cliffs. Many of the paintings have been dated to around 10,000 to 4,000 BCE, but some may be more than 30,000 years old!

This art offers a glimpse into the life of South America's earliest human residents – first, hunter-gatherers and then later, farmers and pottery makers. Images on the walls represent animals, hunting scenes and pictures of dancing figures. Inside one of the oldest sites are the remains of what appears to be a 50,000 year old hearth. Perhaps the paintings on the walls were the stories these prehistoric humans told around a fire.

VATNAJÖKULL NATIONAL PARK, ICELAND

BLUE ICE CAVES

Reaching the spectacular caves deep within Vatnajökull – Iceland's biggest glacier – is no mean feat. First, you must take a bumpy ride in a 'super jeep' across a maze of glacial ridges, before clipping on some crampons to hike in freezing -10°C (14°F) temperatures to the glacier's edge. Then you can begin your descent into the icy tunnels. All is silent but for the eerie crackle of the shifting glacier and the drip, drip, drip of melting ice. Once inside, you'll discover a magical frozen world in vivid hues of blue, from deep indigo to sparkling turquoise.

These ever-changing caves are formed slowly during the warmer months as meltwater flows through the glacier, carving tunnels and chambers into the ice.

LONGITUDE -60°/0°

SENEGAL AND GAMBIA

SENEGAMBIAN STONE CIRCLES

Death is the biggest mystery... and these stone circles in Senegal and Gambia just add to the confusion! Up in the grasslands, rock pillars are arranged in over 1,000 circles around or near burial plots. The bones found inside the circles are laid out in elaborate patterns, but archaeologists are still debating what these mean. In fact, no one really knows who constructed the circles – estimates suggest they could date to anywhere from the 200s BCE to 1500 CE. Such mystery adds to the magical feel, and may have you wondering if they're a gateway to another world. But to the local Senegalese and Gambians it's an ordinary, everyday sort of magic. Often they visit on their way to work to leave a stone atop one of the pillars. Then they'll take a moment to reflect or make a wish, and continue on with their day.

LONGITUDE -60°/0°

IRELAND
FAIRY FORTS

There are more than 40,000 'fairy forts' dotting the landscape of Ireland. According to folklore, these peculiar mounds conceal gateways to the fairy realm – places where these magical beings can move between their world and ours. Legend says bad luck or even death will befall anybody who destroys one – a huge reason why so many have remained undisturbed over the centuries. In fact, these structures are early medieval ringforts – fortified settlements built on circular mounds of earth or stone dating from around the 7th to 12th centuries CE. But who's to say what really lies beneath? Would you dare risk angering the fairies?

Grianán of Aileach in County Donegal is a stone fort, likely built in the 6th or 7th century CE. Might it also be a passageway to the world of fairies?

This painting depicts 'The Riders of the Sidhe' – fairy folk from Irish mythology said to have ruled Ireland in ancient times. They're known for their connection to nature and their magical abilities, including shapeshifting, invisibility and flying.

STAFFA ISLAND, SCOTLAND, UK
FINGAL'S CAVE

Rising out of the ocean on the Scottish island of Staffa, this magical sea cave is formed from enormous hexagonal columns that look like huge hand-crafted pillars. Its striking resemblance to the Giant's Causeway in Northern Ireland inspired an ancient legend. So the story goes, the cave and causeway were two ends of a bridge built by the Irish hero Finn McCool so he could fight the Scottish giant Benandonner. In reality, both sets of columns were formed by intense volcanic activity in this region around 50 million years ago.

Giant's Causeway in Northern Ireland

Over the years, the sea eroded the columns, leaving behind only those in Northern Ireland and Scotland. The cave's impressive acoustics and otherworldly sounds produced by the waves have also made it a popular spot for musicians, including the famed composer Felix Mendelssohn and legendary rock band Pink Floyd.

FEZ, MOROCCO
CHOUARA LEATHER TANNERY

LONGITUDE -60°/0°

Tucked away in a courtyard surrounded by leather shops, you're likely to smell Fez's Chouara Leather Tannery before you see it. To watch it in action, you will need to walk through one of the labyrinthine leather shops to the terrace behind. From there, you can get a bird's-eye view of the tannery below, where workers employ the same traditional techniques for preserving and dying the leather that have been used for a thousand years.

First, the hides are placed in vats containing a pungent mix of water, salt, limestone and pigeon poo to remove the fat, flesh and hair, and soften the skins. Next, they're scrubbed and then placed in vats of dye. The colour depends on the type of plant being used – red from paprika or poppies, orange from henna, blue from indigo, green from mint, and vibrant yellow from saffron. On your way out, you can pick up one of many leather goods on sale – from bags and wallets to jewellery boxes, footstools and babouches (Moroccan pointy-toed slippers).

Vats of pigeon poo and colourful dyes. The droppings are rich in ammonia, which softens the hide and makes it absorbent to dyes.

NEAR LLANES, SPAIN
PLAYA DE GULPIYURI

Standing in the soft sand with the cool seawater washing over your toes, you'd think you were on a beach... except Playa de Gulpiyuri is in the middle of a Spanish field. This tiny body of water is actually a flooded sinkhole, framed by dramatic limestone crags.

A 101m (330ft) tunnel runs beneath the ground all the way to the Cantabrian Sea, which is where the water comes from. You get the best of both worlds: a gorgeous beach but no chance of being swept out to sea!

LONGITUDE -60°/0°

CEREDIGON, WALES, UK
SUBMERGED FOREST

As the tide recedes after a stormy night on Borth Beach, a peculiar sight is revealed. Emerging from the sand are hundreds of petrified tree stumps – the remnants of a prehistoric forest that flourished here some 4,500 years ago. The forest had long been hidden, until a ferocious storm in 2014 exposed this wonder for the first time in possibly thousands of years.

There are some who believe this wasn't just any forest, but part of a long-lost sunken kingdom known as Cantre'r Gwaelod. One story tells how the gatekeeper of this legendary land returned home drunk one evening and forgot to close the gates to the dyke that protected the land from the sea. Waves crashed into the kingdom, and it was lost beneath the Irish Sea... until now, that is.

Layers of peat under the sand have helped preserve the forest, despite years of exposure to strong winds and the sea.

LONGITUDE -60°/0°

DJENNE, MALI
GRANDE MOSQUÉE

This remarkable mosque is the world's largest mud-brick building. It was constructed in 1907, though it is based on the design of a much older Grande Mosquée that once stood on the same site. Built in 1280 by Djenné's King Koi Konboro, it stood for over 500 years until the warrior-king Cheikou Amadou let it fall into ruin in the early 1800s. Today, it dazzles travellers much as it did for centuries. But a structure made out of mud takes a lot of upkeep, and every year after the rainy season, 4,000 local volunteers get to work restoring the mosque.

LONGITUDE -60°/0°

The mosque is built from sun-dried mud-and-straw bricks plastered in clay using techniques passed down from generation to generation.

FALKIRK, SCOTLAND

THE KELPIES

These towering steel horses look like they might rear up out of the earth. Andy Scott's glittering sculptures celebrate Scotland's waterways and industrial history. And while that may seem very modern, the folklore of the Kelpies goes way back. In ancient Scottish myth, kelpies were shape-shifting water creatures. They could take the forms of humans or horses ... and often lured people to their doom. But fear not, these enormous horse heads have more in common with the gentle Clydesdale horses that pulled barges along Scotland's canals than with the fearsome water spirits they are named for.

LONGITUDE -60°/0°

Standing at 30m (100ft) tall, the magical Kelpies are the biggest horse sculptures in the world.

BANDIAGARA ESCARPMENT, MALI

CLIFF DWELLINGS OF THE BANDIAGARA

Travelling through Dogon Country is like walking through the pages of a fantasy novel. The mud-and-rock structures here cling to the cliffs like precarious hobbit-holes. The isolation of the Dogon people isn't by accident. The steep cliffs and slopes of the Bandiagara Escarpment closes Dogon off from the rest of Mali ... and therefore from invasion.

That was a concern centuries ago when the dwellings were built, and is unfortunately still a fear today in Mali's uncertain political climate. But it's easy to forget the outside world as you wander among the elaborately carved doors and straw-roofed storehouses. The fairytale feel of the villages is part of what makes this one of West Africa's most impressive sites.

The traditional mud and stone houses blend seamlessly into the surrounding cliff face.

LONGITUDE -60˚/0˚

KORO, MALI

ANTOGO
FISHING FRENZY

Ah, fishing. Such a peaceful and serene activity – but not in Koro. Though fishing is usually forbidden in this sacred lake, every year the village elders choose a day for the fishermen to gather at the water. The men jostle for position until the elders give a signal. Then they plunge into the water to grab as many fish as they can with their bare hands. It's a mad, crazy, mud-covered dash! Afterwards they bring home their prizes for dinner.

LONGITUDE -120°/-60°

ACCRA, GHANA
KANE KWEI COFFINS

Would you like to spend eternity inside a fire truck, a racing car or a huge wooden hen? At Kane Kwei Carpentry Workshop, you can decide. This coffin-making business was started in the 1950s by carpenter Seth Kane Kwei. Each 'fantasy coffin' is lovingly crafted to reflect the life of the deceased. A musician can be buried in a giant wooden guitar, a fisherman in a boat, or a flying enthusiast in a plane. These unique works of art are deeply connected to traditional Ghanian beliefs about life and death. For the Ga people of Ghana, funerals are celebrations of life rather than sombre occasions and are an opportunity to honour the dead in a personalised way. They also believe the deceased spirit will continue into the afterlife, so these carriages will help serve them in the next world. What would you choose?

LONGITUDE -60°/0°

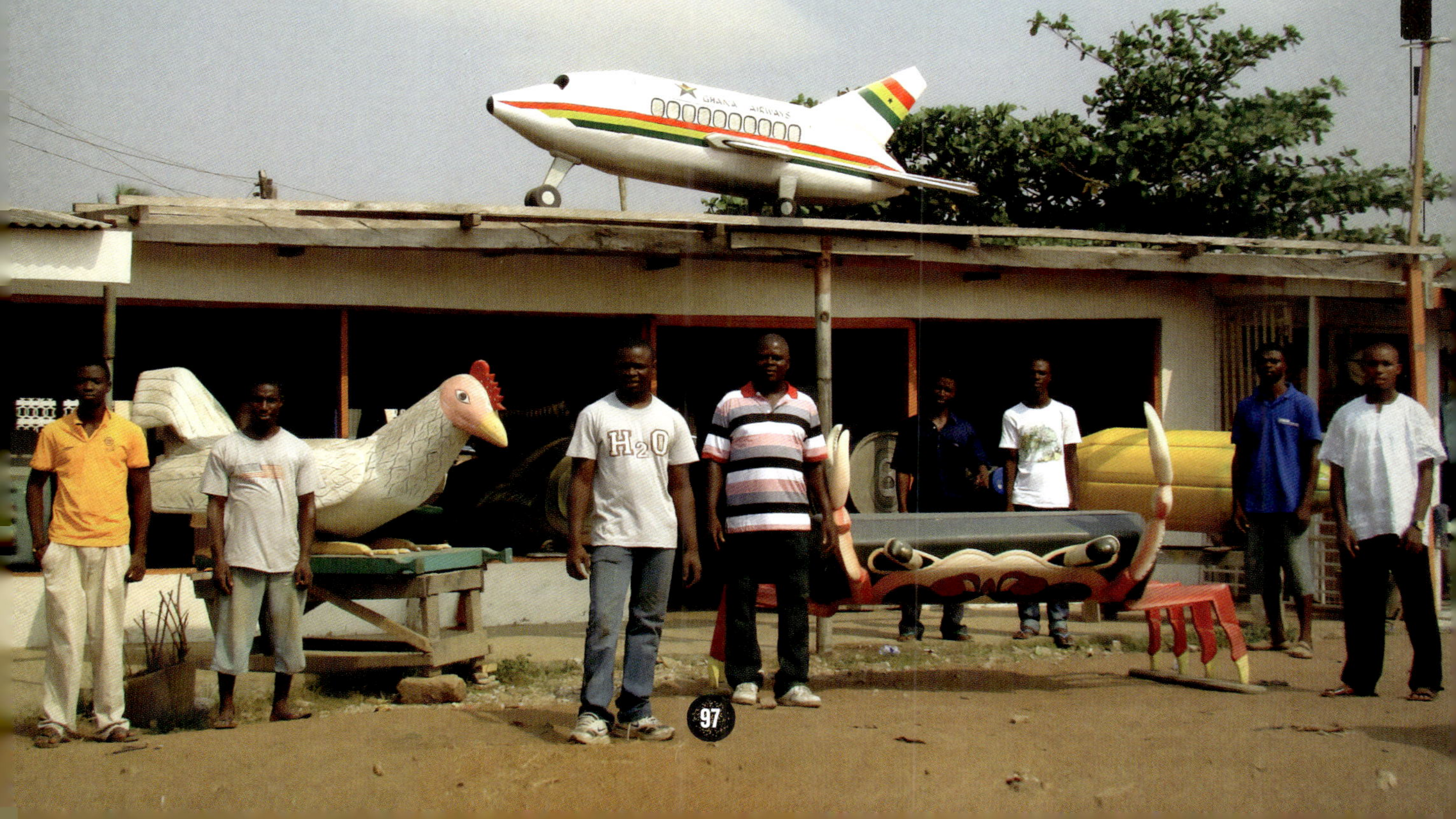

LONDON, ENGLAND, UK
THE MAIL RAIL

LONGITUDE -60'/0°

Squeeze aboard the miniature Mail Rail and discover the history of London's Postal Railway, which lies deep beneath the city's streets! Opened in 1927 to beat traffic congestion, this little-known underground railway was used to shuttle mail between sorting offices using the world's first driverless, electric trains. It stretched 9.5km (6mi) from Whitechapel in the east to Paddington in the west, and at its busiest, it carried some 4 million pieces of mail each day. The Mail Rail stopped delivering mail in 2003, but in 2023, it reopened as a tourist attraction and museum.

The Mail Rail was built for carrying mail, not people, so it's much smaller than a passenger train.

Search for 'baby dragons' in two-million-year-old caves p122

Marvel at lemurs as they leap over knife-like peaks p148

Dare to balance on a rock gripped between towering cliffs p108

Go batty about bats at the world's largest mammal migration p142

Walk in the footsteps of ancient Roman gladiators p116

LONGITUDE 0°/60°

Dance to the drums of a vodún ceremony p103

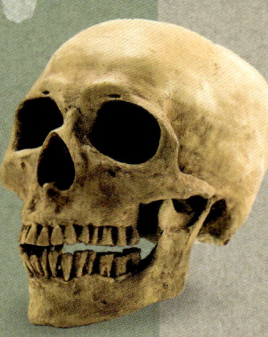

Enter a kingdom of the dead concealed beneath the city streets p104

SAVONNIÈRES, FRANCE
LES GROTTES PÉTRIFIANTES

LONGITUDE 0°/60°

Art takes time, and that's especially true of these 'petrified caves' in the Loire Valley. Place any object (but maybe not one you're really attached to) in the cave's waters, and within a year it will have been turned to stone! The mineral-rich water drips down the walls of the cave, capturing anything in its path and covering it with a glistening stony coat.

The caves themselves are also a work of art. Like an underground goblin kingdom, there are grottos of dangling stalactites and all sorts of rock shapes that have taken centuries to form.

COVE, BENIN

EGUNGUN VODÚN CEREMONY

The drumming begins at dawn. People pour in from across the valley to the village of Cove. They're here for the Egungun Ceremony, which they believe will open a portal for the return of their dead ancestors.

Vodún is a belief system at least 6,000 years old, and more than half of Benin's population practises it. Dancers for the annual Egungun Ceremony wear stunningly decorative costumes that completely hide the person within. As they dance to the drums, they open their souls and bodies to spirits. The ancestors can then look out of the dancers' eyes and see how their descendants are doing. Spectators call out favours of their ancestors, hoping for some help from the beyond.

The dancers twist and whirl as the drums get louder. But spectators must stay back — if they accidentally touch a dancer, it's believed that they can get dragged into the spirit world. Witch doctors stay close in case they need to pull someone back to this world. In this dizzying mix of music, colour and spirituality, it's hard not to get swept away.

LONGITUDE 0°/60°

PARIS, FRANCE
CATACOMBES DE PARIS

Ah, Paris. City of Light, full of romance and... death? Below its lovely boulevards snakes a kingdom of the dead. Damp passageways that run beneath the city contain the bones of an estimated six million people! The problem began at least 250 years ago, when the population of Paris got too big for the cemeteries to handle. After a wall collapsed from the pressure of a mass grave, bodies were placed in what are now the catacombs.

Les Catacombes de Paris were also put to use by both sides during World War II. Both the Nazis and the French Resistance hid in the underground tunnels. A room known as 'Le Bunker' still sports signs in German forbidding smoking and talking.

Visitors should keep their wits about them. Some who go into the tunnels never come out! An 18th-century doorkeeper named Philibert Aspairt disappeared in the tunnels. His body was found 11 years later and had to be identified by the rusty keys on his belt. It's a grim place here for sure, but also filled with the history of an eternal city.

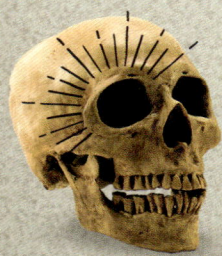

OSOGBO, NIGERIA
OSUN SACRED FOREST

This lush forest contains a meandering river and 40 shrines — many dedicated to Osun, the fertility goddess of the Yoruba religion. Archaeologists believe that people first moved to the grove 400 years ago and settled at this site near the river. But now these woods are the last remnants of primary high forest in southern Nigeria and are known for their diverse wildlife.

Take a walk through the area and you might glimpse a sitatunga antelope (below) or a troop of white-throated monkeys. Gorgeous religious sculptures and temples, both new and old, add to the power of this space.

HAUTERIVES, FRANCE

LE PALAIS IDÉAL

Inspiration can strike in the most unexpected places. One day in 1879, postman Ferdinand Cheval was walking along his mail route when he stepped on a pebble. Cheval picked it up, and an astonishingly ambitious idea was born. The postman decided to build a dreamy palace entirely from the unusual pebbles that he found along his 29km (18mi) route! You can imagine the patience it must've taken him to build his dream. Over the course of 33 years, Cheval created fantastical gargoyles, archways, stairs, elaborate columns and turrets — all out of tiny stones. Next time you trip over a rock, don't be so quick to kick it out of the way.

LONGITUDE 0°/60°

NEAR ØYGARDSTØL, NORWAY
KJERAGBOLTEN

LONGITUDE 0°/60°

Gripped between two towering cliffs high above a fjord (sea inlet) in the Kjerag Mountain, this massive boulder was deposited here by glacial movement around 50,000 years ago. In 1925, it was discovered by avid hiker Thomas Peter Randulff, who took the first known photo of this vertigo-inducing perch.

The name Kjerag, meaning 'shaggy goat hair', is said to come from the small streams tumbling down the craggy cliff face, which resemble the scruffy hair of a young goat.

Today, thousands of adrenaline seekers hike here each year for breathtaking views of the fjord – and the 984m (3,228ft) drop below!

NEAR TYSSEDAL, NORWAY

TROLLTUNGA

Kjeragbolten isn't Norway's only precariously high rock. You can also visit the Trolltunga (Troll's Tongue). This striking rock feature got its name because it reminded people of a Norwegian legend in which a troll, startled by the rising sun, turned to stone with its tongue permanently sticking out. A 12-hour hike out from the village of Skjeggedal brings you to a spectacular vista of sheer cliffs over water. Those who dare can balance on this outcrop for the ultimate photo.

LONGITUDE 0°/60°

HAMBURG, GERMANY
MINIATUR WUNDERLAND

LONGITUDE 0°/60°

You'll wish you were miniature-sized just so you could jump in and wander this sprawling wonderland. The largest model railway in the world, Miniatur Wunderland has it all.

From doll-sized buildings to sports stadiums with teeny-tiny people cheering on their champions, it's just like the real world, but smaller! The City of Hamburg is recreated down to the most minute detail. Miniatur Wunderland was started in 2000 and so far it's taken nearly a million hours to build. But it's not done yet! Big additions are planned, making its future not-so-tiny and bright.

SOUTH TYROL, ITALY

CAMPANILE DI CURON

At first, this looks just like a regular lake... until you notice the campanile (bell tower) rising eerily from its depths. The lake of Reschensee, high in the Alps of northern Italy, was created artificially in the 1950s. Three lakes were converted into one when a dam was constructed.

Kilometres of farmland and dozens of homes were submerged, including a 14th-century church. But the water didn't rise high enough to cover the tall bell tower. When the water freezes, you can even walk out to the tower. There are about 64,000 churches in Italy, but this one may be the most unusual.

LONGITUDE 0°/60°

Some say that on cold, windy nights they can still hear the bells ringing inside the tower, even though they were removed before the village was lost beneath the lake.

THE ALPS, SWITZERLAND
TRIFTBRÜCKE

Don't look down! There's a sheer drop from the cliffs of Trift Gorge straight down to the turquoise waters of Lake Triftsee. But never fear. You're on the Triftbrücke, a feat of Swiss engineering that was built in 2009 and is considered one of the longest and highest pedestrian bridges in the Alps. Just fix your gaze to the stunning beauty of the Alps ahead of you and you'll make it safely across to the other side.

LONGITUDE 0°/60°

SILKEBORG, DENMARK
TOLLUND MAN

Mystery surrounds the story of the Tollund Man. In 1950, his mummified body was discovered 2.5m (8ft) deep in a peat bog in Jutland, Denmark. He was lying, apparently peacefully, in a sleeping position, but tied around his neck was a thick rope. His body was so well preserved, at first it was assumed he had been killed only recently.

In fact, he lived around 405–384 BCE, more than 2,400 years ago! The acidity of the bog preserved the man's bones and soft tissues, including his brain and digestive tract – the contents of his stomach revealed he had eaten fish and porridge as his last meal.

Scientists are still piecing together the details of his life and death. We know he was likely hanged – but was he murdered? An executed criminal? Or was he the victim of sacrifice – an offering to the gods to thank them for the peat, which was used as fuel?

NEAR SKAGEN, DENMARK

RÅBJERG MILE

The Råbjerg Mile just can't stay put. At 40m (130ft) high and with 43 million cubic m (140 million cubic ft) of sand, it's Denmark's largest sand dune. It's part of a conservation zone, but the dune keeps shifting up to 15m (50ft) every year.

In Denmark, shifting sands have driven people out of their homes and even swallowed up buildings. In the 1800s, the Danish government began to buy sand dunes and plant trees to try to stabilise the sand. But when they bought the Råbjerg Mile in 1900, they decided to see what would happen if they just left it alone.

Their experiment backfired because leaving it alone now means that the dunes are seeping out of the conservation zone. But that doesn't seem to bother the birdwatchers and hikers who come here to enjoy its rebellious beauty.

ROME, ITALY
COLOSSEUM HYPOGEUM

Constructed nearly 2,000 years ago for the emperor of the Roman Empire, the Colosseum is one of the most famous structures in Rome and still the largest amphitheatre in the world. Up to 50,000 people could be crammed into this spectacular circular arena to watch gladiatorial combats and wild animal hunts. At times, the arena was even flooded, and naval battles re-enacted.

Lying below the amphitheatre, unseen by spectators, was the hypogeum – an underground complex of halls, cells, tunnels and cages that housed the animals and gladiators before performances. You can walk these corridors and imagine how the unfortunate performers must have felt listening to the roars of the crowd as they awaited their turn.

LONGITUDE 0°/60°

ROME, ITALY
PASSETTO DI BORGO

You may have heard of the Popemobile, a customised bullet-proof car with an elevated seat for the pope's jaunts around the city, but did you know he also has his own personal escape tunnel?

If you look up while strolling through the Borgo district in Rome, you may notice a thick stone wall with archways leading from the Vatican, the official home of the pope, to the fortress Castel Sant'Angelo. Concealed within is a centuries-old secret passage that allows popes to flee their home in times of danger.

Fortunately for recent popes, the escape route hasn't been used for more than 500 years. The last time was in 1527, when Pope Clement VII ran away from 20,000 mutinous troops, who, on the orders of Holy Roman Emperor Charles V, had murdered most of the pope's bodyguards on the steps of St Peter's Basilica.

In 2000, the Passetto (the raised walkway on the left in the picture below) was renovated and opened to the public. So now you can follow in the footsteps of past popes and plot your own escape from invaders.

LONGITUDE 0°/60°

GULF OF PUTEOLI, ITALY

THE SUNKEN CITY OF BAIAE

More than 2,000 years ago, the city of Baiae was a playground for the rich and famous of the Roman Empire. Luxurious villas with mosaic-tiled floors dotted the beachfront, and there were domed bathhouses with saunas and pools. These baths were fed by underground hot springs, thought to have health-restoring powers. Baiae became known by some as 'Little Rome', and rulers such as Julius Ceaser and the emperor Nero had homes there.

But the good times were not to last, and in the 8th century CE, the city was sacked by a Muslim army. Meanwhile, volcanic activity caused the land to subside and Baiae was gradually drowned under the sea – where its remains can still be found. To get a glimpse of this sunken city, you can peer through a glass-bottomed boat, or dive beneath the waves and glide past barnacle-covered statues and elaborately paved (and now very wet) plazas.

LONGITUDE 0°/60°

NOWE CZARNOWO, POLAND

CROOKED FOREST

LONGITUDE 0°/60°

This eerie forest is a mystery. The C-shaped trees here look so unnatural you might wonder if witchcraft was responsible. Some say a heavy amount of snow bent the trees when they were still young. Others say tanks blasted through during a long-ago war and ruined their growth.

But the most likely culprits were some inventive farmers. Trees shaped like this would've been very useful for building ships. Could it be that a clever farmer figured out how to make them grow this way? If so, no one is admitting to it, and the trees are keeping their secret to themselves.

ŽELÍZY, CZECHIA
ŽELÍZY DEVIL HEADS

Hiking through the forested outskirts of Želízy, about 42km (20mi) north of the Czech Republic's capital, Prague, it's startling to see huge stone heads leer out at you. Created in the mid-1800s by Vaclav Levy, a sculptor known more for his work in churches than in forests, these 'devil heads' are definitely much more hellish than heavenly. Worn down over time and covered in moss, they're even creepier to those hiking through the area nowadays than they must have been nearly 200 years ago.

LIKA-SENJ COUNTY, CROATIA

PLITVICE LAKES NATIONAL PARK

LONGITUDE 0°/60°

In the lush beauty of this national park, it's hard to imagine its war-torn past. Waterfalls tumble into bright blue lakes. Butterflies flutter above the water. This stunning place was once a spiritual refuge, where it's said a monk lived in a grotto by the canyon's edge. But during the Balkan Wars of the 1990s, land mines dotted the park. These have since been rooted out, leaving a gorgeous landscape for everyone to enjoy.

The lake is a refuge for many species of rare butterflies, including the Alcon blue (left).

The lake system here is constantly renewing itself: as water washes over the rocks, barriers are formed and then eroded away. In 100 years Plitvice will look completely different from how it does today.

POSTOJNA, SLOVENIA
POSTOJNA CAVES

Dragons are mythical beings… right? You may change your mind after reading about what lives in these caves. Here, ghostly amphibians swim in the underground waterways. When they were first discovered in the 17th century, everyone thought they were baby dragons! In fact, they're a newt-like species called olm or proteus. The caves around this area are the only place on Earth where they live.

While they may not be dragons, these creatures are incredibly special: they can survive up to 10 years without food and they are completely blind. They navigate by feeling for slight electrical fields.

The little dragons have made the caves a famous destination for over 140 years. The ceilings drip with stalactites and limestone rises from beneath to form an underworld cathedral. But the olms are the stars of this attraction. Biologists have been studying their regenerative powers, hoping to find a key to cancer therapies. Who knows what other secrets these not-so-mythical creatures may be keeping?

LONGITUDE 0°/60°

NEAR SICILY, ITALY
STROMBOLI

This very lively volcano is a ferry journey away from the island of Sicily. One of the most active volcanoes on Earth, it has been nearly continuously spewing lava for the past 2,000 years. Because of this, ancient sailors nicknamed it the 'Lighthouse of the Mediterranean,' though perhaps you'd want to sail your ship guided by something a little less fiery!

Today, visitors can hike across the lower part of the volcano's bare and ashen landscape or experience the volcano's fireworks from the sea with a sunset boat tour around the island. As you gaze up, you'll see smoking craters at the summit steadily hiss steam and occasionally spew jets of ash and lava, while molten rocks tumble down the slopes into the Mediterranean 914m (3,000ft) below.

LONGITUDE 0°/60°

NAMIBIA

WILD HORSES
OF THE NAMIB DESERT

No one knows exactly how this herd of wild horses came to be living in the inhospitable sand dunes of the Namib Desert. Are they descended from cavalry horses abandoned by the German Imperial Army in 1915? Were their ancestors shipwrecked here en route to Australia from Europe? Baron Captain Hans-Heinrich von Wolf had a castle a hundred kilometres from here in 1909, but his widow abandoned it after he was killed in World War I. Considering he owned thoroughbreds, were these horses let loose from there to the wilds of the desert? Whatever their origin, the sight of them racing across the vast, barren expanse is magical to behold.

SVALBARD, NORWAY

GLOBAL SEED VAULT

LONGITUDE 0°/60°

Built deep inside a frozen mountain, the vault is designed to withstand earthquakes, rising sea levels and explosions.

Whoever dreamed up Norway's Global Seed Vault has definitely seen their share of disaster movies. This remote outpost in the Arctic houses crop seeds – enough so that if disaster strikes, humankind can rebuild (or replant, as it were).

There are around 1,700 seed outposts around the world, but this one provides the ultimate backup plan: more than 1.3 million seed samples from almost every country around the world. They're all kept safe in little sealed bags in this far-flung station, which is halfway between Norway and the North Pole.

Seeds can only be reclaimed by the country that put them there. And based on its security systems, the Vault's creators were also watching James Bond movies. Not content that the location itself is secure, the creators put in place extreme safeguards against both natural and human-made disasters. The Vault was built to stand the test of time – and a zombie apocalypse.

CENTRAL CEDERBERG, SOUTH AFRICA

WOLFBERG ARCH

You have to crawl, scramble, balance, and squeeze yourself through caverns to get to this natural wonder. The 4-hour hike to the Arch passes through the Wolfberg Cracks, a series of splits and fractures carved into the cliff face. Then it flattens into a majestically beautiful landscape... and little shade.

The Wolfberg Arch is a natural formation here that seems as if it's sculpted out of the rock — totally worth every sore muscle when you lay your eyes on it.

LONGITUDE 0°/60°

BAJINA BAŠTA, SERBIA
DRINA RIVER HOUSE

This tiny house is perched on a rock in the middle of Drina River. It was built in the 1960s by local youths who dreamed of a blissful escape from the noisy world. Though the house has been rebuilt many times due to damage from flooding, it's still a beautiful and peaceful place. Seeing this miniature sanctuary emerge from the mists — defying gravity atop its rocky base — could make anyone want to leave the world behind too.

LONGITUDE 0°/60°

This curious wooden house is the perfect spot for relaxing and swimming.

JUODKRANTE, LITHUANIA
WITCHES' HILL

LONGITUDE 0°/60°

Don't worry: none of the witches and wizards here will hurt you. Over 70 wooden figures line this open-air sculpture garden, and they're both charming and creepy. There are totem poles topped with dragons, there's a chair carved with ancient faces, and a witch's-tongue slide in the playground. You might need to leave a trail of breadcrumbs to find your way out!

BELOGRADCHIK, BULGARIA
KALETO FORTRESS

You could be forgiven for walking right past the Kaleto Fortress without seeing it. The citadel blends into the rocks on the northern slope of the Balkan Mountains. And this wasn't a mistake. The building's camouflage made it an ideal stronghold for over 200 years, starting in the late 1100s. From the ramparts, you would have been able to see an enemy army marching towards you across the hills. Today, you can wander among the rocks and wonder at all the years of history they've seen.

LONGITUDE 0°/60°

STOB, BULGARIA

STOB PYRAMIDS

It's like these sandstone towers belong on another planet. Near Stob village, lush meadows end and orange dusty landscapes begin where these pyramids rise almost 12m (40ft) above jagged cliffs. Scientists say the otherworldly landscape was created by wind and snow. But local villagers tell a different story. Legend has it that during a wedding the best man kissed the groom's bride-to-be. The shock petrified the guests right then and there.

LONGITUDE 0°/60°

If you look closely, you will notice that some of the rocks appear to be wearing hats!

NEAR ŠIAULIAI, LITHUANIA
HILL OF CROSSES

Back in the 19th century, locals started laying crosses on this hill to honour loved ones killed in a rebellion. Over the years, what started as a small monument has grown to over 100,000 crosses! Soviet authorities bulldozed the site in 1961, but under cover of night, locals crept to the hill to lay more crosses. When the KGB (the Soviet Committee for State Security) blocked the road and marked the area as quarantined, the faithful still kept coming, and the hill grew higher and higher.

When Lithuania finally won independence in 1990, the hill became a symbol of freedom and victory. People could lay their crosses openly, and so they do. The hill keeps growing every day.

LONGITUDE 0°/60°

NIEU-BETHESDA, SOUTH AFRICA
OWL HOUSE

Great art can rise from the depths of despair, and the Owl House in South Africa is one such example. Helen Martins was unhappy in life, and poured her sadness into art, creating figures out of concrete. The figures come in both real and fantastical forms: mermaids, animals, farmers, religious scenes, and of course the trademark owl from which the house gets its name. Many are brightly painted or decorated with colourful glass. In the face of bad fortune, Martins created something truly special.

MAKGADIKGADI PAN, BOTSWANA
KUBU ISLAND

This remote corner of the planet seems touched by a magic wand. Kubu Island rises from the world's largest network of salt flats. Twisted baobab trees are backed by a horizon that seems to stretch on for forever. Though the landscape is dry now, five centuries ago, there was a huge inland lake surrounding the island. Hippos wallowed in the shallows of that lake, and it's from them that Kubu gets its name: kubu means hippopotamus in the local Setswana language. It's easy to feel connected to the people who once lived here. There are stones and tools left here by ancient people, and not much has changed on Kubu Island since then.

LONGITUDE 0°/60°

LOPĂTARI, ROMANIA
LIVING FIRES

Watch your step as you pick your way across the plains of Lopătari. The land here is covered with fires that burst out from the soil! Natural gas smoulders beneath the surface, fuelling the flames that shoot out through cracks in the earth. When darkness falls, the expanse fills with orange and blue flames that look like they come from the underworld. But the Romanians have a more cheerful view of this place locally known as Focul Viu (Living Fires). They say the purifying fires protect wildlife and bring good fortune to those who visit.

LONGITUDE 0°/60°

RUOKOLAHTI, FINLAND
KUMMAKIVI

LONGITUDE 0°/60°

Local legend has it that this huge 500-tonne boulder was placed upon a smaller rock in the middle of a forest by giants or trolls (who are immensely strong and have a tendency to move boulders around). Scientists will tell you it was moved by glaciers after the last ice age some 11,000 years ago. It looks as though it is precariously balanced and with a strong push could topple – but as visitors soon discover, it is sat firmly in place. Do you think you could budge it?

MATOBO, ZIMBABWE
MATOBO NATIONAL PARK

A common agama, also known as a rainbow agama

The unusual rock formations have been shaped by weathering over millions of years, but local beliefs suggest they are the remains of ancestors – frozen for eternity by powerful forces. If a boulder falls, they say, it is a bad omen.

LONGITUDE 60°/120°

Entering this World Heritage–listed park is like stepping into a dreamland. There are huge boulders that seem to teeter against one another, rainbow-coloured lizards, ancient rock art, bright lichen, and soft vegetation. It's no wonder this place is sacred to the Indigenous Ndebele people.

Today, they still come here to perform ancient rituals such as the rainmaking ceremony – traditional songs and dances performed before the start of the rainy season or during a drought to pray for rain.

The park is also home to critically endangered black rhinos, and the largest population of leopards in Africa. You may think you're dreaming, but this is the African wilderness at its most awe-inspiring.

DENIZLI, TURKEY

PAMUKKALE-HIERAPOLIS

These enticing basins of clear blue water are contained in chalk-white trays of travertine, a calcium carbonate rock. The water is the temperature of a perfect bath and rich in minerals, which may explain why there has been a spa here since Greco-Roman times.

On the hillside above the water are the ancient ruins of the city of Hierapolis. A huge outdoor amphitheatre is evidence of the wealthy community that once existed here. From the pools to the ruins, it's easy to imagine a day in the life of the ancient people who once lived here.

LONGITUDE 0°/60°

VIRUNGA MOUNTAINS, DEMOCRATIC REPUBLIC OF CONGO

NYIRAGONGO

LONGITUDE 0°/60°

What starts out as an ordinary hike through the forest soon turns into an extraordinary ascent to the mouth of a volcano. The vegetation thins out and the soft ground becomes a brittle field of black lava. Nyiragongo's last eruption was in 2002, and you can still see the remnants of that eruption the higher up the mountain you climb. Take shelter for the night right under the rim and watch the sky turn red from its fiery smoke. It's nature in its most magnificent — and terrifying — glory.

KASANKA NATIONAL PARK, ZAMBIA

BAT MIGRATION

LONGITUDE 0°/60°

Between October and December, 10 million golden fruit bats swarm into the tiny Mushitu swamp forest in Kasanka National Park. If you were to walk the forest floor during the day at this time of year, you'd be strolling underneath a massive canopy of sleeping bats. As the Sun sets, the forest comes to life. From all around, the bats take flight, winging off into the dark.

WHITE DESERT, FAIYUM, EGYPT

WADI AL-HITAN (WHALE VALLEY)

As you stand on the parched sandstone rocks in this spot in Egypt's Western Desert, it's hard to imagine that this was once home to an abundance of colossal prehistoric sea creatures. But around 40 million years ago, the area was submerged by a sea and was the hunting grounds for sharks, crocodiles... and walking whales! Fossils discovered here in 1989 turned out to be a species called *Basilosaurus isis*, an ancient ancestor of modern whales that had four legs, feet and toes, and could walk on land – albeit slowly and clumsily!

Today, hundreds of skeletons remain half-concealed in the sand. To get a glimpse of these prehistoric beasts, you must first travel by four-wheel-drive, by camel or by foot, across unmarked desert sands and behind a mountain known as the 'Mountain of Hell'. No mean feat!

LONGITUDE 0°/60°

RIVER NILE STATE, SUDAN

PYRAMIDS OF MEROË

Most people have heard of the pyramids of Egypt, but directly south, marooned in the orange deserts of Sudan, are the relatively unknown Pyramids of Meroë. Smaller and steeper than their famous Egyptian counterparts, these extraordinary structures are equally awe-inspiring.

They were built from 800 BCE to 350 BCE for the kings and queens of Kush, a powerful kingdom in Nubia (present-day northern Sudan and southern Egypt) – long after the Egyptians had given up pyramid building.

Like the pharaohs of Egypt, the Nubian rulers were mummified and buried with a wealth of treasures, including gold necklaces, weapons, and items of furniture, for use in the afterlife. But rather than being contained within the pyramid itself, the burial chambers were concealed beneath them – some as deep as 20m (65ft) below the surface. Over the years, many of the treasures have been plundered, but the pyramids remain as breathtaking monuments to a once mighty civilisation.

LONGITUDE 0°/60°

The light-coloured pyramids shown here are modern reconstructions to show what they once looked like. The darker coloured ones are the original ancient pyramids.

CAPPADOCIA, TURKEY
DERINKUYU

Walking among the pink and gold hillsides of Cappadocia is like entering another world. Rising out of the earth are hundreds of 'fairy chimneys' – rocky pillars with mushroom-shaped tops that have been sculpted over millennia by the wind and rain. Even more surprising is what lies beneath – over 200 vast underground cities that were a place of refuge from invaders for nearly 3,000 years.

The biggest can be found at Derinkuyu. Adapted from ancient caves and carved into the soft volcanic rock, this 18-level hidey-hole extends nearly 85m (280ft) deep and could shelter up to 20,000 people. Inside were living quarters, storage rooms, wine and oil presses, a church, stables for livestock, and even a well – all locked away behind heavy boulder doors that could be rolled closed in times of danger. The subterranean cities were finally abandoned in 1923, but today, you can descend into the narrow, musty tunnels and explore the maze of corridors and dwellings without fear of invasion!

TSINGY DE BEMARAHA NATIONAL PARK, MADAGASCAR

THE FOREST OF KNIVES

The name 'Tsingy' in the local Malagasy language means 'where one cannot walk barefoot'... you just have to look at the jagged limestone pinnacles, rising 100m (300ft) above deep canyons and river gorges, to see why. Unless you're a lemur, of course! These nimble-footed primates are endemic to Madagascar, meaning they are found nowhere else in the world, and are perfectly adapted for the island's unique landscape. Using their long limbs to propel themselves, and their tails for balance, they dart across the razor-sharp rocks with ease.

Intrepid travellers can journey by pirogue (traditional wooden canoe) through the glorious Manambolo River Gorge, then explore the needle-like peaks using the system of rope bridges and walkways. Just try not to look down!

LONGITUDE 0°/60°

The jagged peaks were formed over millions of years by monsoon rains and wind. They are the perfect refuge for lemurs, away from natural predators and humans.

IRAN
PIGEON TOWERS

Most of us want to avoid pigeon poo as much as possible. But not the builders of these towers in Iran. Their sole purpose was to collect pigeon excrement, and the more the better. Back when the towers were built in the 17th century, pigeon poo was used as fertiliser for farming. In order to keep their fields healthy, farmers needed the stuff, and often.

The solution was to build these towers. Known as dovecotes, they're specifically designed for pigeons to live and do their business in. The towers have hundreds of holes in them so pigeons could land, rest, and deposit their droppings. Since the poo was contained in one space, it was easier to gather without wasting a single precious drop. The method was so effective that thousands of these towers were built across Iran.

They were also used in Egypt, Scotland, France and the Baltics. But Iran's are probably the most impressive. The towers are actually quite pretty and stylish... if you don't know what is inside.

LONGITUDE 0°/60°

SOCOTRA, YEMEN
DRAGON BLOOD TREES

Isolated for millions of years, the island of Socotra is filled with unique plants and animals that exist nowhere else on the planet – like the bottle tree that stores water in its bulbous trunk, the Socotra giant gecko, or the rare and beautiful Socotra sunbird. Its most iconic – and weirdest – species is the dragon blood tree, named for the blood-red sap that oozes from its trunk when cut.

Ancient Greek, Indian and Arabian travellers sought out this peculiar sap, believing it to be the blood of dragons and that it had medicinal and magical properties. It may not really be dragon's blood, but it has long been a valuable commodity, used and traded by the local people as a dye and a remedy for digestive problems and wounds. Today, the tree's survival is under threat from cyclones that batter the island and overgrazing by goats, but locals are working hard to protect these precious natural marvels for generations to come.

LONGITUDE 0°/60°

In Greek mythology, the dragon blood trees sprang up on the site where the hero Heracles slayed the 100-headed dragon Ladon that guarded a sacred grove of golden apple trees. When cut, the tree bled Ladon's blood.

YAZD, IRAN

ZOROASTRIAN TOWERS OF SILENCE

No sound but the desert wind and the occasional cry of a vulture echo through the Towers of Silence. It's eerie for sure, and even more chilling when you know their purpose.

Built in the 16th and 17th centuries by practitioners of the ancient religion of Zoroastrianism, the Towers are where they came to bury their dead. Inside low stone houses, bodies were carefully washed and prepared. Then the dead were laid out in circles and left in the open for carrion birds to feed on. Once the bones were picked clean, they were lovingly placed inside the towers, known as ossuaries.

Although the Towers of Silence are now empty and unused, Zoroastrianism is still practised today in Iran, India and across the rest of the world, though there are very few sects left that still observe this particular death ritual. The Towers of Silence now sit quietly, filled only with the ghosts of their past.

LONGITUDE 0°/60°

BAT, OMAN
BAT & AL AYN TOMBS

Everyone assumes that these brick structures are ancient tombs. The trouble is, none of them contain any bodies and there's no proof they ever did. The structures are 5,000 years old and shaped like beehives. Perhaps they were temporary tombs, or maybe they were something different entirely — we may never know. What we do know is that the structures form a striking silhouette against the mountain behind them.

Maybe it was the stark beauty of the rock face that inspired an ancient civilisation to build them here, probably unaware that their origin would later remain a mystery.

KARAKUM DESERT, TURKMENISTAN
DARVAZA GAS CRATER

This crater is nicknamed the 'Door to Hell', and it's clear why – temperatures within this blazing pit can soar to 1,000°C (1,830°F). Roughly the size of a football field, the crater is surrounded by a vast, bleak landscape. Though it might seem like a freak occurrence in nature, the crater is actually human-made.

In 1971, Soviet engineers were hoping to strike oil in this spot, but their rig collapsed into a gas pocket. Worried that the methane gas would be dangerous, they set it on fire to burn the gas off. They thought it would burn out within a few weeks... but nearly 50 years later, it's still on fire.

Go in search
of ancient civilisations p180

Sniff out
the world's biggest
(and smelliest)
flower p190

**Don't forget
your sunglasses**
at this dazzling
temple p168

Pray at a church
that looks like a dove
... or a chicken p184

Step inside a temple
where 25,000 sacred
rats scamper across the
grounds p160

LONGITUDE 60°/120°

Snack on bugs
at a creepy-crawly
market p174

There's no place like gnome
at this town built just for gnomes p188

Descend into purgatory
at this recreation
of Buddhist hell p181

HINGOL NATIONAL PARK, PAKISTAN

PRINCESS OF HOPE

Rising high above the sweeping deserts of Hingol National Park, the Princess of Hope gazes out as if she's surveying her kingdom. The statue looks like it was carved by a skilled artisan, and it was – wind and rain. The powerful forces swirled together to create a natural wonder: a stone tower that resembles a woman in a flowing dress.

LONGITUDE 60°/120°

ASTANA, KAZAKHSTAN
BAYTEREK MONUMENT

This soaring tower looks futuristic, but was inspired by an ancient tale. According to Kazakh legend, a mythical bird laid a golden egg at the top of a sacred tree. The egg contained the secret to happiness but it was too high up in the tree for humans to reach.

At Bayterek, however, the egg can be reached... by elevator! Travel up the white tree-shaped tower to the shimmering glass orb all the way at the top. Even if you don't find the secret to happiness there, you'll get amazing 360-degree views of the city from the observation deck.

The Bayterek Tower's 'egg' is not actually made of gold. It is made of glass that appears golden in the sunlight.

LONGITUDE 60°/120°

BIKANER, RAJASTHAN, INDIA

KARNI MATA TEMPLE

Rats rule at Karni Mata. There are rats on the floors, rats on the stairwells, rats wriggling along handrails and skittering in every nook and cranny. But don't call an exterminator – these furry rodents are meant to be here! They are thought to be the reincarnated children of Karni Mata, the Hindu warrior sage for whom the temple is dedicated.

Inside the temple, the walls echo with the squealing of the 25,000 rats that live there. Devoted pilgrims feed the animals out of their hands and kiss their tiny pink noses. Huge trays of milk and ceremonial food (called *prasad*) are laid out as offerings to the rats. It's considered a blessing to eat the food after the rats have already nibbled on it. Here they are not pests – they are sacred beings.

Worshippers take part in a ceremony at Karni Mata temple. Daily rituals involve prayers and offerings of food to the goddess Karni Mata and the temple's rats.

THE MALDIVES
THE SEA OF STARS

With powder-soft white-sand beaches and colourful underwater worlds thriving in its coral reefs, the Maldives is a dream destination. But visit the reefs during the later summer months, and you'll discover an even more amazing spectacle. As night descends, the water is illuminated by millions of shimmering blue lights – as if stars have fallen from the sky and scattered into the ocean.

This dazzling display is caused by tiny bioluminescent creatures called plankton. As the plankton are disturbed by the movement of the waves, they light up – a clever defence mechanism designed to startle or confuse predators. If you dip your toes into the twinkling waters, the colour intensifies, allowing you to create your own mini universes beneath your feet.

LONGITUDE 60°/120°

ALMATY REGION, KAZAKHSTAN

SINGING DUNES OF ALTYN-EMEL NATIONAL PARK

Have you ever heard a sand dune sing? The sound can vary from a deep, gentle hum (similar to an organ) to a booming roar that can travel for miles. This remarkable natural phenomenon occurs when dry sand is disturbed by the wind, and the millions of tiny grains collide and vibrate. There are several singing dunes around the world, but some of the most tuneful are those in Kazakhstan's Altyn-Emel National Park.

To make one hum, climb to the top then slide or sand board down its slope to create a mini avalanche. Get your friends and family to join in and create your very own desert concert. Just make sure you wait for dry weather – the dunes never sing when it rains!

LONGITUDE 60°/120°

KOLSAI LAKES NATIONAL PARK, KAZAKHSTAN
LAKE KAINDY

The creation of this lake was a series of unfortunate events that ended up giving us something pretty special.

LONGITUDE 60°/120°

Lake Kaindy has a long and dramatic history. An earthquake in 1911 triggered a massive limestone landslide in these mountains, which in turn created a dam – and left this pristine lake. The water glows like jewelled turquoise, its vibrant colour the product of limestone deposits.

Spruce trees rise like spears out of the water, hinting at the submerged forest below. Although they died long ago, the trees have been perfectly preserved in the lake's chilly waters. The surreal sight of a sunken forest in the crystal-clear waters make this a popular destination for scuba divers.

BIKANER, INDIA

MEGHALAYA TREE BRIDGES

LONGITUDE 60°/120°

The Indian state of Meghalaya is one of the wettest places on the planet. During the monsoons, torrential rains leave villages surrounded by water. Luckily, the locals have developed an ingenious way of dealing with these epic rainfalls. For centuries, they have trained the aerial roots of Indian rubber trees to form bridges across flooding rivers. Hollow tree trunks are positioned to help the roots grow. Once they are strong enough, they are braided into a 'living bridge' that can support the weight of 50 people! The bridges start to look like they grew naturally right out of the forest.

MON STATE, MYANMAR (BURMA)
KYAIKTIYO PAGODA

Giving new meaning to the phrase 'defying gravity' this 7m (23ft) tall boulder seems like it's about to topple from the edge of its rocky perch. Only a tiny part of it touches the bedrock. Is it science or something more? Legend has it that a single strand of the Buddha's hair prevents the 'Golden Rock' from toppling off the ledge.

That tale has made this one of Myanmar's most sacred pilgrimage sites. Every part of the boulder has been lovingly painted with gold leaf. A golden shrine, known as a stupa, sits on top like a crown. Buddhist pilgrims travel from all over just for the chance to add their own glittering gold leaf to the rock as a sign of their devotion.

But the journey here isn't easy. Pilgrims hike just under 11km (7mi) up a hard trail barefoot. Non-pilgrim visitors can keep their shoes on and ride up in rickety trucks along a bumpy road. The reward is a magical vista, especially at sunset.

LONGITUDE 60°/120°

ZHANGYE DANXIA NATIONAL GEOPARK, CHINA

RAINBOW MOUNTAINS

LONGITUDE 60°/120°

You won't have to run fast to chase a rainbow at this geopark. All the rainbows here are earthbound, and they never fade away. A masterpiece 20 million years in the making, these mountains shine with bands of bright colour. Geological movement has pressed the sandstone into what looks like a layer cake dyed with several shades of food colouring. Over time the sandstone has eroded into pillars and other shapes. The extreme desert heat split the rock, forming valleys of creeks and cliffs. During sunrise and sunset the hills blaze scarlet and gold. And after a rainstorm the colours are even brighter.

The multicoloured landscape is like a piece of artwork, as painted by nature.

JOHOR BAHRU, MALAYSIA

ARULMIGU SRI RAJAKALIAMMAN

You'll need sunglasses in this sanctuary of glittering beads and glass. The story goes that while Guru Bhagawan Sittar sat wondering how to rebuild one of the city's oldest temples in the 1990s, he was struck in the eye by a ray of light. He discovered that the light came from the reflection of a glass artwork more than a mile away, which is when inspiration struck. He then created the temple using multicoloured beads and glass mosaics, and hung chandeliers to set light bouncing off every surface. Every single bead on the walls is engraved with a prayer, and the mosaics are made from more than 300,000 pieces of glass! It's sparkle taken to a whole new level.

GOBI DESERT, MONGOLIA
FLAMING CLIFFS

Looming large out of the Gobi Desert, the so-called Flaming Cliffs of Bayanzag glow a fiery orange or red during the golden hours of sunrise and sunset. But it's what hidden within that makes this a truly remarkable place – one of the richest collections of dinosaur remains. Among its treasures have been the first dinosaur eggs ever found. They were discovered here in the 1920s and provided the first proof that dinosaurs were egg-laying creatures.

Close-up view of fossilised dinosaur eggs

This geological wonder is best viewed at sunrise or sunset when its colours are at their most vibrant.

LONGITUDE 60°/120°

YUNNAN PROVINCE, CHINA
FUXIAN LAKE

LONGITUDE 60°/120°

For 1,750 years, Fuxian Lake kept its secret hidden. Then in 2001, divers discovered an ancient city covered in moss lying in ruins deep in the lake. Divers found mystical symbols carved into stone, animal-like masks, and ritual objects carved with the Sun and Moon. Scientists carbon-dated the ruins to approximately 260 CE, but the mystery of who lived here and how the city ended up underwater is still unknown. Perhaps it will be another 1,750 years before the lake gives up that secret too.

SINGAPORE
HAW PAR VILLA

This surreal sculpture garden is populated with over a thousand statues painted in vivid, glossy colours. Some are nightmarish: a crab with a man's head or a girl with a snail's body. Others are dreamy: magnificent dragons and uplifting scenes of meditation. This introduction to the world of Chinese religion and mythology was built by brothers Aw Boon Haw and Aw Boon Par. They wanted to portray the idea of traditional Chinese moral values: do good deeds and you'll be rewarded, but do bad deeds and you'll be punished. The whimsical statues capture these important values of Buddhism and other Chinese religions.

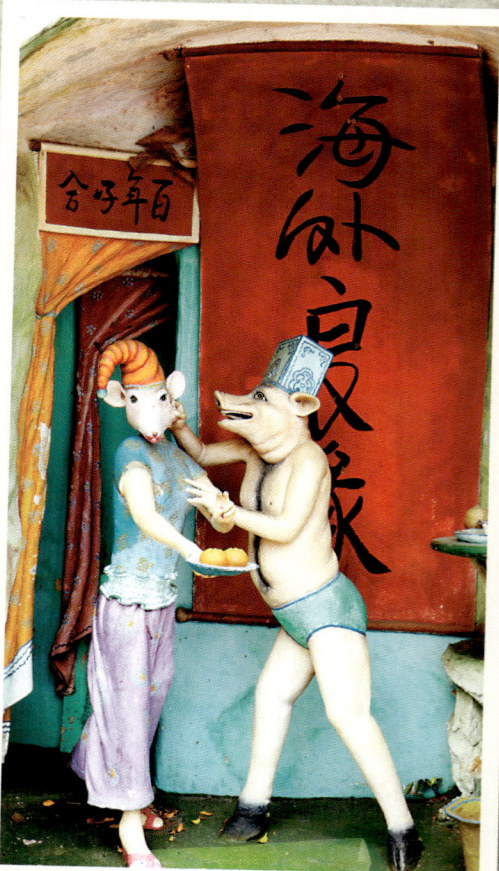

SIEM REAP, CAMBODIA
TEMPLE OF TA PROHM

LONGITUDE 60°/120°

Just a stone's throw away from the world-famous Angkor Wat temple is another, more secretive ruin – Ta Prohm. Built from 1186, it was once a thriving monastery and centre of learning. It housed thousands of people and its magnificent buildings were decorated with intricate carvings, precious stones and gold. But around 500 years ago, after the collapse of the mighty Khmer Empire, it was abandoned, and the sacred site was slowly swallowed by the jungle. Today, its tumbling towers are gripped by the twisted roots and branches of strangler fig trees. Its maze-like corridors are covered in creeping lichen, and fallen stone Buddha statues litter the floor. This atmospheric scene is thought to be very much like how the famous monuments of Angkor would have looked when European explorers first stumbled upon them. Luckily for Ta Prohm, conservation efforts have kept nature at bay, but if left untouched, there's no doubt the jungle would devour it once more.

BANGKOK, THAILAND
CREEPY-CRAWLY MARKETS

Here's something you might not expect to see on the menu: bugs. At Bangkok's street food markets and night markets vendors sell a whole variety of creepy-crawly treats! You can try pretty much anything that can be found under a rock: crickets, water bugs, spiders and even scorpions. You can have them served raw, or fried in peanut oil for a crispy crunchy texture!

Insects and other creepy crawlies are becoming an increasingly popular foodstuff across the world. You never know, one day you may find that you have a taste for tarantulas and crickets.

LONGITUDE 60°/120°

NEAR SIEM REAP, CAMBODIA

KBAL SPEAN

The rushing water here can't hide the site's real draw: carvings of Hindu gods above and below the waterways. Vishnu reclines with his wife Lakshmi by his feet. Brahma sits regally on a lotus flower. A waterfall tumbles over monkey-headed Hanuman. It's believed that hermits sculpted the images as early as the 10th century CE.

To get here, you've got to make your way through the forest, hanging onto branches and tree roots to get uphill. You can miss a lot of the carvings because many are concealed by overgrown trees and waterfalls. But once here, you'll want to explore every nook and cranny of this hidden wonder.

LONGITUDE 60°/120°

Water cascades over sculptures of Hindu gods at Kbal Spean.

SIBERIA, RUSSIA

OLKHON ISLAND

If the name Siberia makes you think of a bleak landscape of ice and snow, think again. The sun-warmed island of Olkhon is a peaceful, beautiful place on Lake Baikal. It is home to the Buryats: Indigenous people who believe the island to be a spiritual place. In the thick forest on the northern side of the island, every rock and oddly shaped tree is hung with a colourful cloth. This marks the place as an *oboo*, or home to a kindly spirit. Each natural landmark on the island has a special significance to the Buryats. To them, it makes sense that their benevolent spirits chose this welcoming island as their home.

LONGITUDE 60°/120°

CHRISTMAS ISLAND, AUSTRALIA

RED CRAB MIGRATION

At the start of the rainy season, one of nature's most striking events takes place here. Tasting the first drops of rain, countless bright red crabs crawl out from underground burrows in the island's central forests. Creeping sideways, they make their way to the beach, which can be up to 8km (5mi) away. Soon, the slow trickle of crabs becomes a tide of millions,

What's their rush? They've got to find their soulmate! Propelled by instinct, these little creatures stick to a tight schedule. Female crabs must reach the burrows dug by the males on the coast, woo and mate. After mating, the females incubate their eggs in a brood pouch for about two weeks before shimmying into the waves and releasing their eggs into the water, where the eggs hatch. Around a month later, the young, fully formed crabs emerge from the ocean (as long as they haven't been eaten) and begin their own epic journey inland to the forests.

During the crabs' mass march across the island, local rangers patrol the streets with plastic rakes, scooping the critters out of harm's way from bikes, cars and trucks. But dodging traffic isn't the worst of it. The tough little crabs must scale steep cliffs, scuttle over jagged rocks and fight off hordes of angry yellow ants. With all these dangers, you can understand just how impressive their ritual is.

Adult crabs searching for their soul mates on the beach

Baby crabs emerging from the sea to begin their journey back to the forests

KARYAMUKTI, INDONESIA
GUNUNG PADANG

LONGITUDE 60°/120°

This unusually-shaped hill scattered with mysterious stone columns has become the subject of fierce debate. Some scientists claim that the hill hides the remains of a human-made pyramid built up to 27,000 years ago! If this were true, it would make this the oldest pyramid in the world, predating others, including those of Egypt, by many thousands of years, and imply the existence of a lost ancient civilisation.

Most experts have debunked this theory, saying the mound is a natural structure, formed from an extinct volcano, with human adornments on top that date to around the 2nd–8th century CE.
What do you think?

Is Gunung Padang the world's oldest pyramid?

NEAR DA NANG, VIETNAM
AM PHU CAVE

Decorated to represent the Buddhist ideas of purgatory and hell, this cave carries a harsh moral message about what happens if you give in to evil. The sunlit top of Thuy Son, the 'marble mountain' in which the cave is located, represents the heavens. From there, you descend down 10 levels, each painted with vivid scenes of gruesome punishment for evildoing. After this frightening trip, you can climb a steep staircase back up to the light. You'll definitely behave after having this taste of hell!

Thuy Son – the 'marble mountain'

LONGITUDE 60°/120°

NEAR HOI AN, VIETNAM
MY SON

Beneath Da Voi (Cat's Tooth Mountain) lie the ruins of the ancient Champa kingdom, which thrived here from the 4th to the 13th century. Its kings and queens are buried at My Son, where 18 temples dedicated to the god Shiva still stand. Though nature has been slowly taking over the site, you can still see carvings of Hindu legends on the buildings.

The kingdom was largely forgotten until 1898, when it was rediscovered by French scholars. The crumbling temples were restored in the 1930s, but during the Vietnam War (1955–75), the site suffered extensive damage during a single week of bombings by the US. It's still standing, though – resilient even through war.

LONGITUDE 60°/120°

The temples are decorated with intricate carvings of Hindu gods and goddesses, and animals such as lions and elephants.

NEAR MAGELANG, INDONESIA

GEREJA AYAM

In 1990, Daniel Alamsjah felt a divine calling to build a house of worship for all faiths. He decided to construct it in the shape of a dove, the everlasting symbol of peace. If you tilt your head and use your imagination, it could look like a dove. But the crown on the top of its head and the open red beak definitely make it look more like a rooster. Unfortunately the building was never finished, and the place was abandoned in 2000.

Now it's been downgraded from both a dove and a rooster, and is just referred to as the 'Chicken Church'. Moss covers the outside, like green feathers. The tail is crumbling and sections are covered in graffiti. The building has decayed so much that it's in danger of collapse. Perhaps soon this dove will fly away to make its nest somewhere else.

LONGITUDE -120°/-60°

NEAR BEIJING, CHINA
ZHENGBEI TOWER

LONGITUDE 60°/120°

Within the wonder that is the Great Wall of China, there is a forgotten stretch of the wall you can explore. If you break away from the better-known sections, you can wander off to the quiet village of Xizhazi. Climb up an ordinary path between cornfields and farmhouses. Pass sleepy dogs and ramshackle chicken coops. Hike through the woods until you get to a wall of brick and white stone. Then pick your way up a haphazard staircase, and you'll be inside a Ming Dynasty watchtower.

The world spreads out below you from this high-up perch. The mountains to the west rise and fall like a roller coaster. From the upper battlements of the Zhengbei Tower, you can imagine yourself as a warrior long ago, your bow and arrow pointed down at any enemy who dared to attack.

Though this far-flung part of the wall is crumbling and overgrown, you can still picture what it must have been like hundreds of years ago. This Great Wall saw wars start and end, empires rise and fall.

ZHEJIANG PROVINCE, CHINA
LONGYOU CAVES

For ages, people thought Longyou's ponds were bottomless. But in 1992, some curious locals decided to drain them to figure out just how deep they really were, and discovered more than they bargained for: a vast system of human-made caves.

There are 36 grottos, stretching out over 28,000 sq m (300,000 sq ft). Every chamber is decorated with the exact same pattern of straight lines. Fish, birds, animals and scenes of ordinary ancient life are also chiselled into the sandstone.

The water was pumped out of the caves, and now the sunlight spills in from the open skylights, illuminating this wondrous underground discovery.

Scientists can't pinpoint when the caves were built, but their best guess is around 200 BCE. Who created the carvings and why is a mystery. One theory suggests the caves were a re-creation of the constellations that their builders saw in the sky above them. Whatever the truth may be, the Longyou Caves are keeping quiet about it, for now.

WESTERN AUSTRALIA

GNOMESVILLE

Once upon a time, a garden gnome appeared in the hollow of a tree at this roundabout. But the gnome was lonely. Sympathetic townspeople placed other garden gnomes next to him so he would have some company. And thus, a village – and a major tourist attraction – was born. Gnomesville has grown to a population of at least 5,000 gnomes! The gnomes come from all over the world, as visitors flock here to bring their own garden gnomes to this sanctuary. There are gnomes of every design: partying gnomes, plane-flying gnomes, and even a gnome sitting on a toilet. If the gnomes misbehave, they go to the fenced-in 'Gnome Detention Centre'. Signs around Gnomesville proclaim, 'Gnome Wasn't Built In A Day' or 'Better Gnomes & Gardens'. If you've got a garden gnome, why not consider relocating it to Gnomesville? After all, there's no place like Gnome.

KALIMANTAN, BORNEO, INDONESIA
RAFFLESIA FLOWER

You'd think that the world's largest flower would be a delight to behold… and it's certainly an extraordinary sight. This enormous reddish-brown bloom with polka dots can grow to 1m (40in) across and emerges proudly from the forest floor. But don't stand too close: the flower is notorious for its terrible odour – a potent blend of rotting meat and stinky feet.

This may not sound good to you, but it's considered a real treat for visiting flies and beetles that are attracted by the smell and help pollinate the plant. Incredibly rare and difficult to find, the flowers last only a week before wilting away, and you'll need to venture deep within the rainforest to catch a glimpse (and whiff) of this pungent marvel.

KOMODO NATIONAL PARK, INDONESIA
KOMODO DRAGONS

Measuring up to 3m (10ft) long, with scaly skin, sharp claws and huge muscular tails, these giant lizards are the planet's only living dragons. These aren't the flying, fire-breathing beasts of ancient myths and legends, but they do have serrated shark-like teeth and saliva that secretes venom into their prey. They live on just a few islands in Indonesia, including their namesake, Komodo Island. They are an endangered species, making them a rare and awe-inspiring discovery for brave visitors who venture into the tropical forests of Komodo.

But beware! Komodo dragons can smell blood from several kilometres away, so be sure to cover any wounds before stepping foot on the island and stick with your guide at all times. The dragons have been known to attack wayward travellers if they feel threatened or are especially hungry!

These firece predators will eat almost any kind of meat, from insects and birds to deer, pigs, smaller dragons, and even water buffalo. Male dragons will also often fight each other over females or territory.

LONGITUDE 60°/120°

Walk among stars washed up on a beach p203

Take a peek at Japanese snow monkeys bathing in hot pools p214

Marvel at microbes at this museum of good bacteria p199

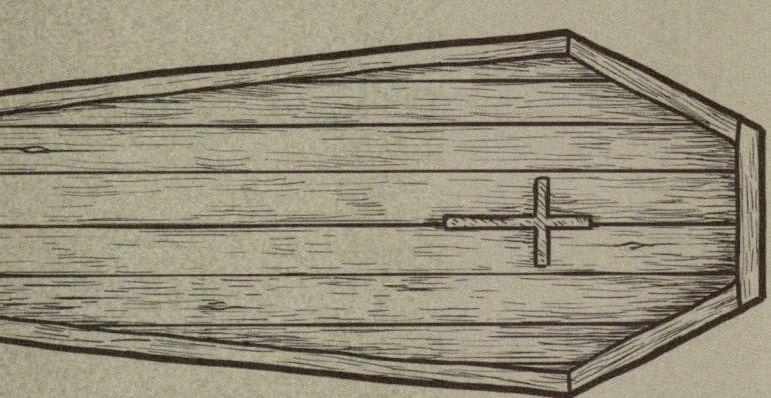

Look up at a cliff of hanging coffins p194

Creep through overgrown vines in an island ghost town p200

Paint the town at this rainbow village p198

LONGITUDE 120°/180°

Dive beneath the waves ... and post a letter at an underwater post office p222

Taste new flavours at a festival of wild foods p227

SAGADA, PHILIPPINES
ECHO VALLEY HANGING COFFINS

Looking up at the cliffs on the mountainous island of Luzon, you'll find coffins hanging down the rock face. The island is populated with the Indigenous Igorot people, and their open-air cemeteries are a blend of spiritual and practical. The Igorot believe that the higher up the coffins are, the closer they are to the spirits of their ancestors. Igorot elders actually build their own coffins, and after they die, their bodies are smoked and wrapped tightly in cloth.

They are then carried to the cliffs in a procession of honour and stakes are driven into the cliff to hold the coffins in place. The practical side of the hanging coffins is that they are kept safe from scavenging animals, floods and – in rougher times – grave robbers.

The practice of hanging coffins is slowly dying out as the older population of Igorots passes on. But these unique cemeteries are likely to endure for generations to come.

WESTERN AUSTRALIA, AUSTRALIA
LAKE BALLARD

Shimmering under the Outback sun, this salt lake appears like a mirage in the middle of a barren landscape. Look closer and you'll notice a set of deep-set tracks. Follow these to the lake, and you'll see 51 tall metal statues along the way.

It's the world's largest outdoor art gallery, created by Antony Gormley. The sculptures represent the 51 residents of the nearest town, Menzies. Walking in and out of cloud shadows, your eyes will trick you. Is the lake right in front of you or still a good distance away? The eerie figures aren't telling.

LONGITUDE 120°/180°

WESTERN AUSTRALIA, AUSTRALIA
LAKE HILLIER

LONGITUDE 120°/180°

If you were going to draw a lake, you'd probably use your blue pencil – unless you're drawing Lake Hillier, which is bright, bright pink! No one knows why this body of water, so close to the blue Southern Ocean, is the colour of bubble gum. The rosy hue may be caused by the same type of bacteria that makes some other lakes pink, though this has never been confirmed. One thing is for sure: the water from Lake Hillier stays pink even when you scoop it into a bottle. You can't visit the lake since it's part of a restricted wilderness preserve, but you can take a helicopter tour over it for a view of all its pink glory.

TAICHUNG, TAIWAN

RAINBOW VILLAGE

Fearful that his fading village would be destroyed, former soldier Huang Yung-Fu picked up a paintbrush and set to work. He began by painting a tiny bird on his bedroom wall to keep him company. Then he kept on painting. Soon, his colourful art of animals, flowers and Chinese figures covered all the walls in his bungalow before spilling outside into the streets and onto every building. Nicknamed 'Grandpa Rainbow', his efforts paid off: locals saved the town from demolition, and now it's on its way to being designated a cultural landmark.

LONGITUDE 120°/180°

Grandpa Rainbow was 86 when he began painting his village with images inspired by his childhood. It was the first time he'd picked up a brush since he was a child.

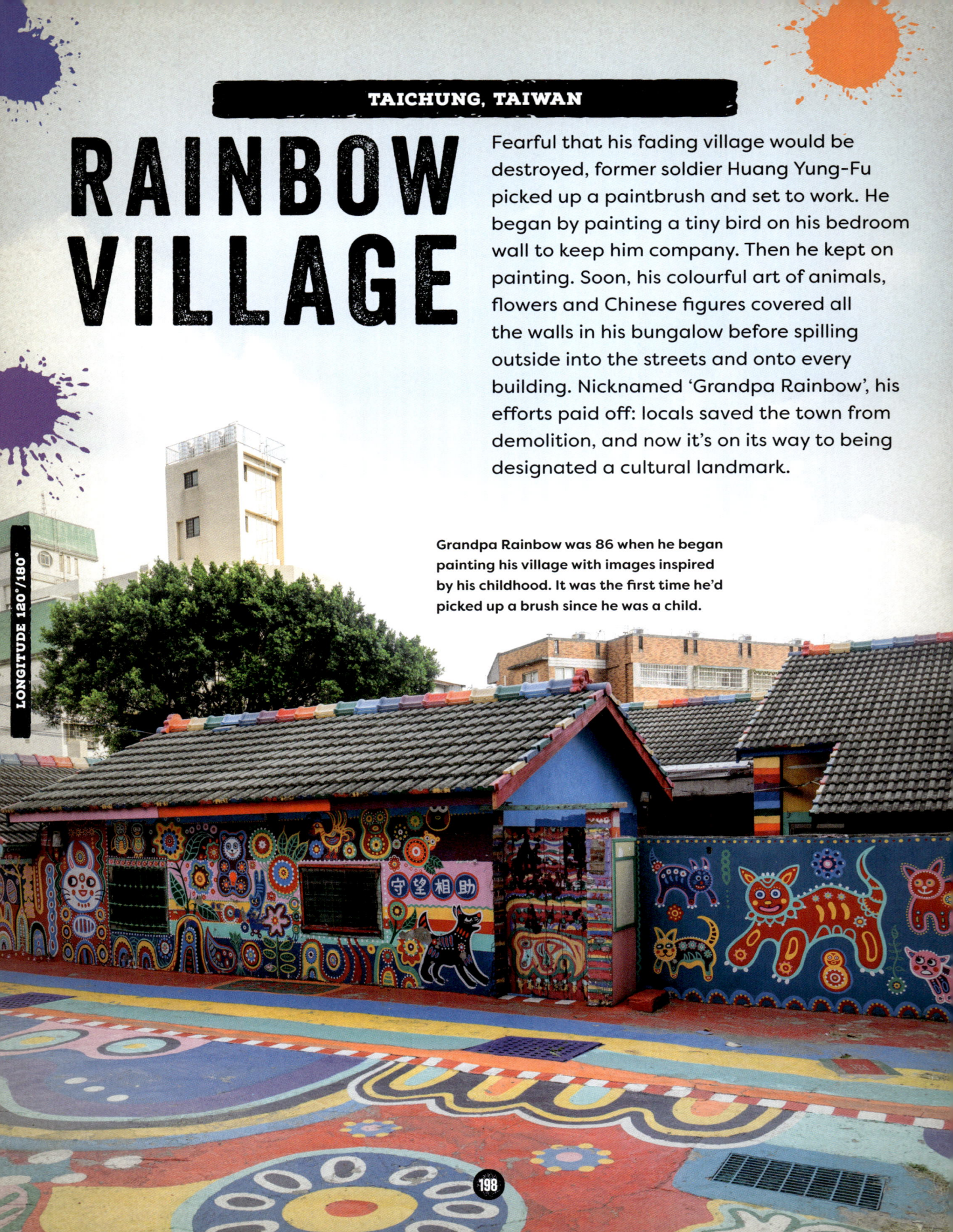

YILAN, TAIWAN

BENEFICIAL MICROBES MUSEUM

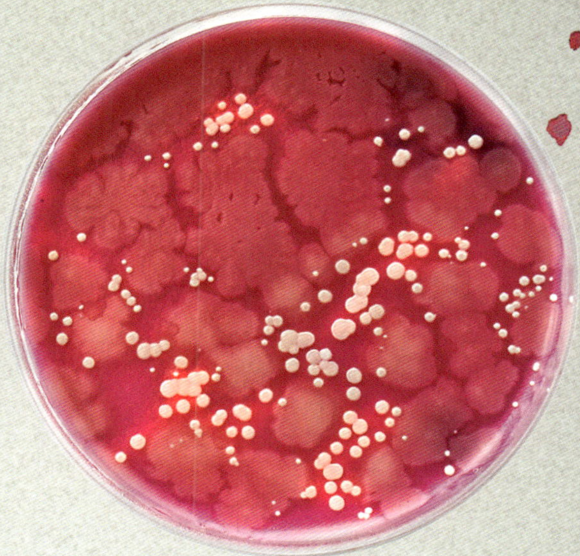

Put away your hand sanitiser. Here, bacteria are celebrated. The goal of this Taiwanese museum is to help people understand all the good that bacteria do for us. It teaches people about friendly microorganisms and which bacteria are harmful. There's a workshop on fungus and skincare experiments. Even germophobes will surely leave with a newfound respect for the bacteria soldiers that protect our bodies every day.

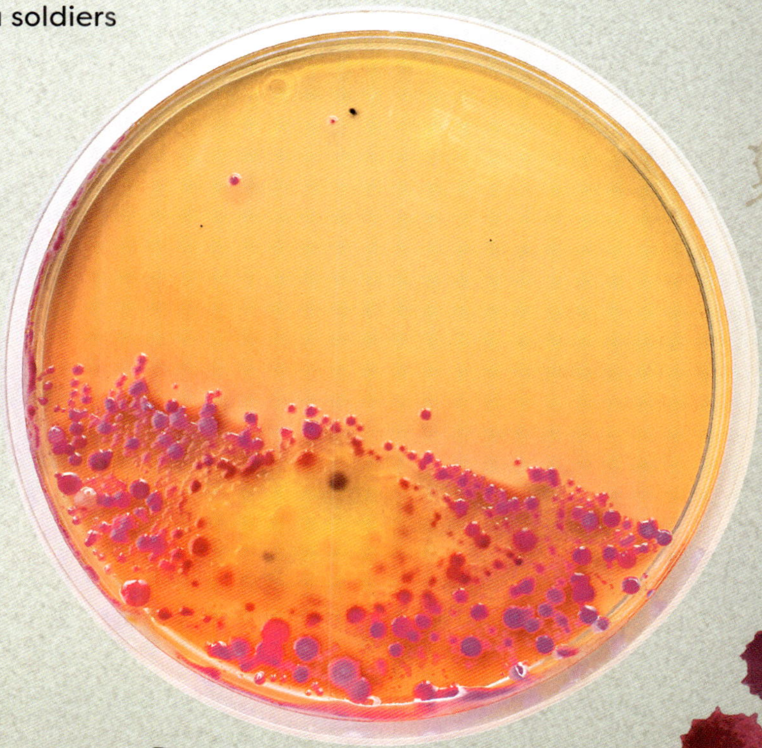

LONGITUDE 120°/180°

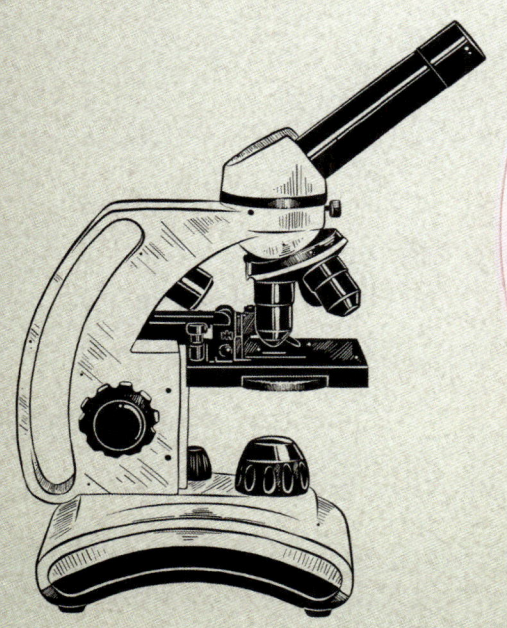

SHENGSHAN ISLAND, CHINA

HOUTOUWAN

Halfway between creepy and magical is this island ghost town. A once-busy fishing village, its people drifted away over the years to find jobs in the big cities. Now, there are only a few elderly residents left, and nature has taken over the town.

Peek into a crumbling house and you'll see furniture coated in dust. Try to climb a staircase and you'll have to fight through overgrown vines. The desolation might be a little eerie, but the greenery that has swallowed up much of the village is what makes this place so special.

LONGITUDE 120°/180°

NARA, JAPAN

NARA PARK

We often think of deer as shy animals, but that's not true of the sika deer that roam the town of Nara. Legend has it that a god rode into town on a white deer in the 8th century, and ever since then, deer have ruled the roost. The animals are considered treasures, and they're pretty much allowed to do anything here. They'll wander through shops, restaurants and even some residents' houses! Some have even learnt to bow to ask for food and say thank you – a sign of respect in Japan. Just make sure you only offer them the crackers sold by local vendors, as they are made especially for deer.

JEJU ISLAND, SOUTH KOREA
HAENYEO

Don't believe in mermaids? You may change your mind after meeting the women divers of Jeju Island in South Korea. Known as 'Korea's mermaids', the haenyeo dive so deep into the cold ocean that they seem to defy the laws of nature... or at least human lung capacity! The diving tradition is passed down from mother to daughter. They start training young so that by the time they're ready to dive, they can hold their breath for up to 3 minutes at a time.

While mining treasure such as seaweed, octopus, abalone and sea urchins is their mission, they've also been witness to the changing ocean. Because of pollution, the abalone they seek are becoming increasingly rare. And the tradition is dying out. Many daughters choose to leave Jeju to seek their fortunes in the big city.

Today, the oldest haenyeo are over 80 years old, and most are over 60 years.

LONGITUDE 120°/180°

IRIOMOTE ISLAND, JAPAN
STAR-SAND BEACHES

On a few remote beaches in Japan, you can hold the stars in your hand. Legend has it that the star-shaped grains of sand are the children of the stars in the sky. Really, they're the exoskeletons of tiny sea creatures. The creatures wash up on shore by the millions, especially after sea storms. Sadly, overeager merchants are scooping up the unique sand and bottling it to sell to tourists faster than the sand can replenish itself. So visitors should remember to admire the stars in the palms of their hands, and then let them go so the next visitors are able to hold the stars too.

LONGITUDE 120°/180°

CHINA AND NORTH KOREA

HEAVEN LAKE

LONGITUDE 120°/180°

This bright blue lake does indeed look heavenly, as its name suggests. Situated at the top of Mt Paektu, it's located in the caldera of a volcano, which is a hollow crater created by large eruptions of magma over a short period of time. Though this volcano on the Chinese and North Korean border is still active, the lake is peaceful. But rumours of what lies beneath are not so serene. Since 1903, there have been sightings of the 'Lake Tianchi Monster'. Early descriptions are of a buffalo-like creature. More recent reports are of a strange beast with a long neck and human-like head. In 2007, a local filmmaker shot a grainy film that appears to show seal-like creatures frolicking in the water. According to the filmmaker, they had long fins (or perhaps wings) and could swim as fast as yachts! Perhaps Scotland's Loch Ness Monster has an Asian cousin.

GANGNEUNG, SOUTH KOREA

NORTH KOREAN SUBMARINE

Undercover meant underwater on this North Korean submarine. It carried 26 North Korean spies into South Korean waters in the autumn of 1996. Their mission was to gather information about South Korea's navy, then return to the submarine and glide away underwater without ever being discovered. This didn't quite go as planned. The submarine ran aground and the crew could not free the boat.

They burned all the secret documents onboard and fled back to North Korea on foot. Only one of them possibly made it back: the others were all captured. And the submarine is still stuck in the same spot where the spies left it. Now you can visit the spy sub and creep through rusting metal corridors in Gangneung Unification Park. There are even scorch marks on the wall from when the sub's commander destroyed their secrets.

LONGITUDE 120°/180°

EIL MALK ISLAND, PALAU

JELLYFISH LAKE

If you're after a wet and wild adventure, dive into the warm turquoise waters of this 12,000-year-old lake and snorkel alongside millions of golden jellyfish. Don't worry – they don't sting. Each day, they migrate in huge swarms across the lake following the direction of the Sun as it rises in the east and sets in the west, before descending into deeper waters at night.

These sun-loving creatures aren't just soaking up the rays for fun: the sunlight 'feeds' the algae that lives deep inside their tissues, which in turn gives the jellyfish energy. Because they get most of their food from the algae, they have little need to sting for food. You can swim so close to them, you can watch as they open and close their umbrella-shaped bodies and propel themselves gracefully through the water.

LONGITUDE 120°/180°

These friendly jellyfish range in size from ping-pong balls to bowling balls. By following the path of the Sun, they also avoid predatory sea anemones that lurk in the shadows around the edge of the lake.

SOUTH AUSTRALIA, AUSTRALIA
COOBER PEDY

LONGITUDE 60°/120°

Coober Pedy is no ordinary town. It is, quite literally, a town beneath your feet. What drove the people underground? Coober Pedy is the world's largest supplier of opal stones. Deep shafts lead down to mines where the gemstones are collected. The majority of residents live under the ground in human-made caves dug into the hillsides. The dugouts maintain a comfortable temperature year-round, unlike the sweltering outback weather above ground. Homes, churches and shops are all carved out beneath the earth.

There is one attraction located above ground: a grassless golf course. The course is all dirt except for a little piece of artificial turf that golfers carry around with them to tee off from. And for some who find the daytime heat too much to handle, you can play golf at night with a glow-in-the-dark ball. This surreal landscape is the one golf club where 'Keep Off The Grass' signs aren't needed!

Above: The kitchen of a dugout home
Right: Opal seams sparkling within the rock

NORTHERN TERRITORY, AUSTRALIA

INJALAK HILL, WEST ARNHEM LAND

A visit to Arnhem Land is like stepping back in time. This vast region in Australia's Northern Territory is owned by the area's Aboriginal peoples, and thanks to their guardianship, it remains a wild and breathtakingly beautiful place, with towering escarpments, deep gorges, lush eucalyptus forests and alligator-filled rivers.

Rising from the red, dusty landscape, in a remote area that can be cut off for months in the wet season, is Injalak Hill. Here, etched in the rocks are hundreds of rock paintings – some as old as 10,000 years.

The paintings were made over the course of thousands of years, showing different styles and techniques over time. Among them is the distinctive 'X-ray' style art, which shows the internal organs and bones of animals and spiritual figures. Local guides will also recall Dreaming stories of how the landscape and its inhabitants came to be. At the nearby Arts and Crafts centre, you can witness local artists at work using knowledge and techniques passed on through their ancestors.

The rock paintings at Injalak Hill offer a window into the life of its Indigenous inhabitants.

EAST ARNHEM LAND, NORTHERN TERRITORY, AUSTRALIA

GARMA FESTIVAL

Set in a small clearing in a pristine forest of eucalyptus trees, the Garma Festival is a four-day celebration of the ancient customs of the Yolngu – one of the many Aboriginal groups of Arnhem Land. Stretching back more than 60,000 years, theirs is one of the oldest living cultures on the planet.

Non-Indigenous visitors are welcome to join the gathering and learn about the Yolngu through their songs, stories and art. Each day ends with a ceremonial dance called a *bunggul*, accompanied by the deep hum of the *yikadi* (didgeridoo).

Bunggul dances tell the Dreaming stories of the Yolngu, which have been passed down from generation to generation over thousands of years.

LONGITUDE 120°/180°

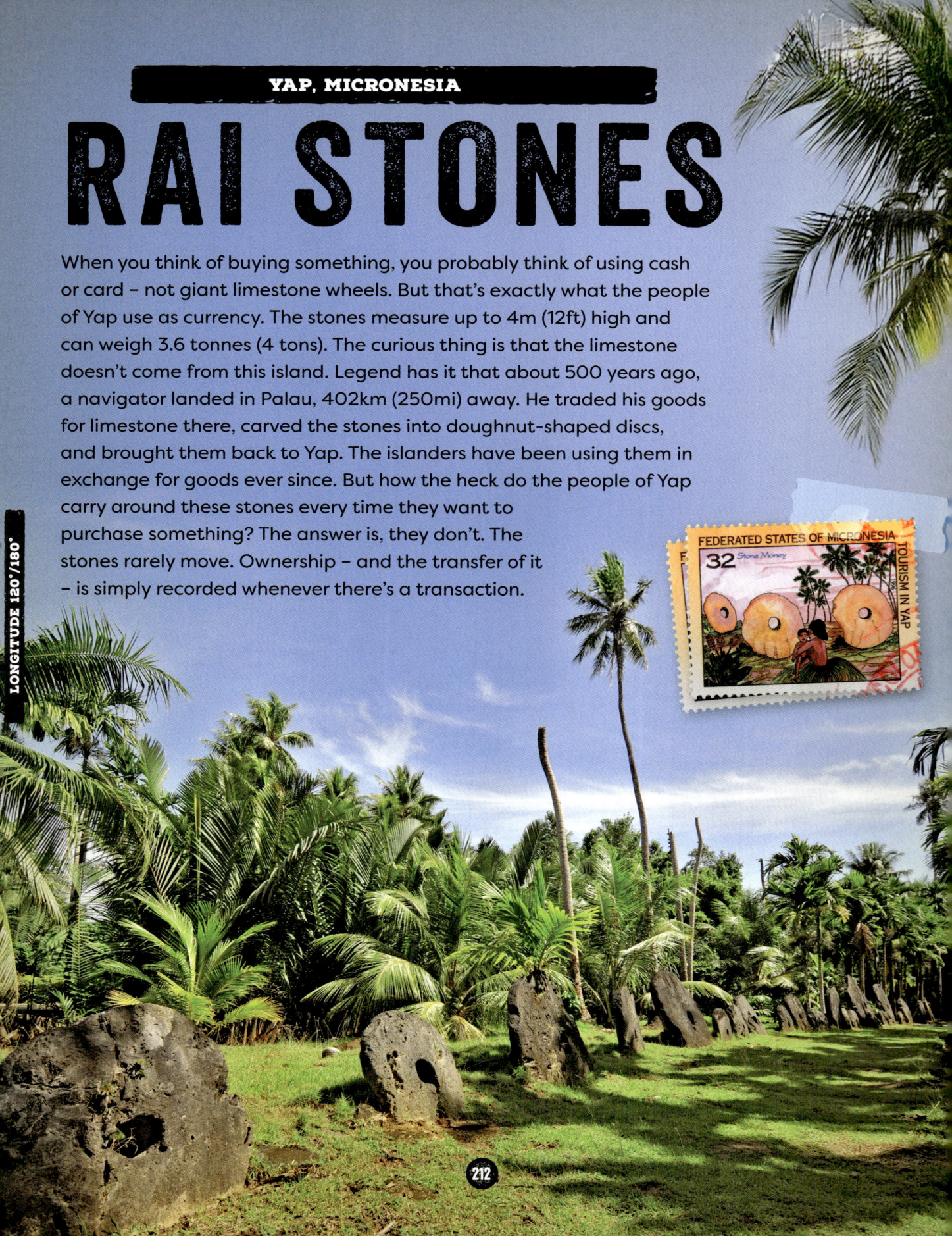

YAP, MICRONESIA
RAI STONES

When you think of buying something, you probably think of using cash or card – not giant limestone wheels. But that's exactly what the people of Yap use as currency. The stones measure up to 4m (12ft) high and can weigh 3.6 tonnes (4 tons). The curious thing is that the limestone doesn't come from this island. Legend has it that about 500 years ago, a navigator landed in Palau, 402km (250mi) away. He traded his goods for limestone there, carved the stones into doughnut-shaped discs, and brought them back to Yap. The islanders have been using them in exchange for goods ever since. But how the heck do the people of Yap carry around these stones every time they want to purchase something? The answer is, they don't. The stones rarely move. Ownership – and the transfer of it – is simply recorded whenever there's a transaction.

LONGITUDE 120°/180°

PAPUA, INDONESIA
KOROWAI TREE HOUSES

Hundreds of years before the first skyscrapers, the Korowai people built towering treetop homes in the remote, swampy rainforest of southeastern Papua – all without modern materials and tools. In the 1980s, some Korowai began moving to ground-level or stilt homes in villages, but many clans still build and live in treehouses deep in the forest. Here, they hunt for wild pigs and other animals, fish in the rivers and gather fruit and vegetables.

Some 6m (20ft) above the ground, their lofty homes are made using only materials from the surrounding forest. The wood-framed walls are lashed together with rattan palm (vine-like) ropes and covered with palm bark – no nails required! The roofs are made by weaving together large forest leaves. To reach their front doors, the Korowai climb a long ladder made from a tree trunk carved with notches. Amazingly, these remarkable structures are built in a matter of days but can last for years.

Living off the ground once provided safety from neighbouring rival peoples and offers protection from flooding and wild animals.

JOSHINETSU KOGEN NATIONAL PARK, JAPAN

JIGOKUDANI MONKEY PARK

LONGITUDE 120°/180°

Monkeys do have a lot of human habits ... including soaking in a nice hot bath. In the cold winter months, troops of Japan's macaques (also known as 'snow monkeys') emerge from the forests to warm up in the steaming waters of the hot springs that bubble up from the frozen ground. The scene is much like the one at the nearby Kanbayashi Onsen, where human bathers come to relax in the geothermally heated pools. The sweet red-faced monkeys have also been seen enjoying another familiar human activity: having a snowball fight!

People in Japan have been bathing in hot springs, known as *onsen*, for at least 1,300 years. The monkeys followed suit at Jigokudani when the park was created in the 1960s.

TASHIROJIMA, JAPAN
CAT ISLAND

Cat lovers, rejoice! There is an entire island devoted to your favourite feline friend. On Tashirojima Island, cats outnumber people six to one. They're believed to be lucky, and keeping them as pets is considered bad taste. So the wild cats roam the island as they please. But don't worry. Taking care of the cats is also thought to bring good fortune, and so these cats are very well taken care of.

Tashirojima was made rich by silk and fishing over the centuries, and the cats were a big part of both. Cats were encouraged to chase mice away from silkworms, keeping the worms safe to spin their silk. Later, fishermen kept the cats happy by feeding them from their daily haul. Now the human population of the island is dwindling, and the cats are taking over, so there's plenty of room for you to move in and live out your ultimate cat-crazy dream.

LONGITUDE 60°/120°

NEW SOUTH WALES, AUSTRALIA

GIANT PINK SLUGS OF MT KAPUTAR

On a remote peak 1,500m (4,885ft) above sea level live some vividly coloured little creatures. This is the only place in the world where you can find them. They are bright neon slugs! The slugs come in various shapes and colours. Some are as long as a cucumber and hot pink, while others are triangular and bright red. After it rains, these guys crawl out from their underground lairs to feast on lichen and tree moss. They live in the remains of an extinct volcano, which was active 18 million years ago. Have the slugs been around that long? Scientists aren't sure. However long they've existed, their dazzling colours are captivating visitors who don't mind getting the creepy-crawlies.

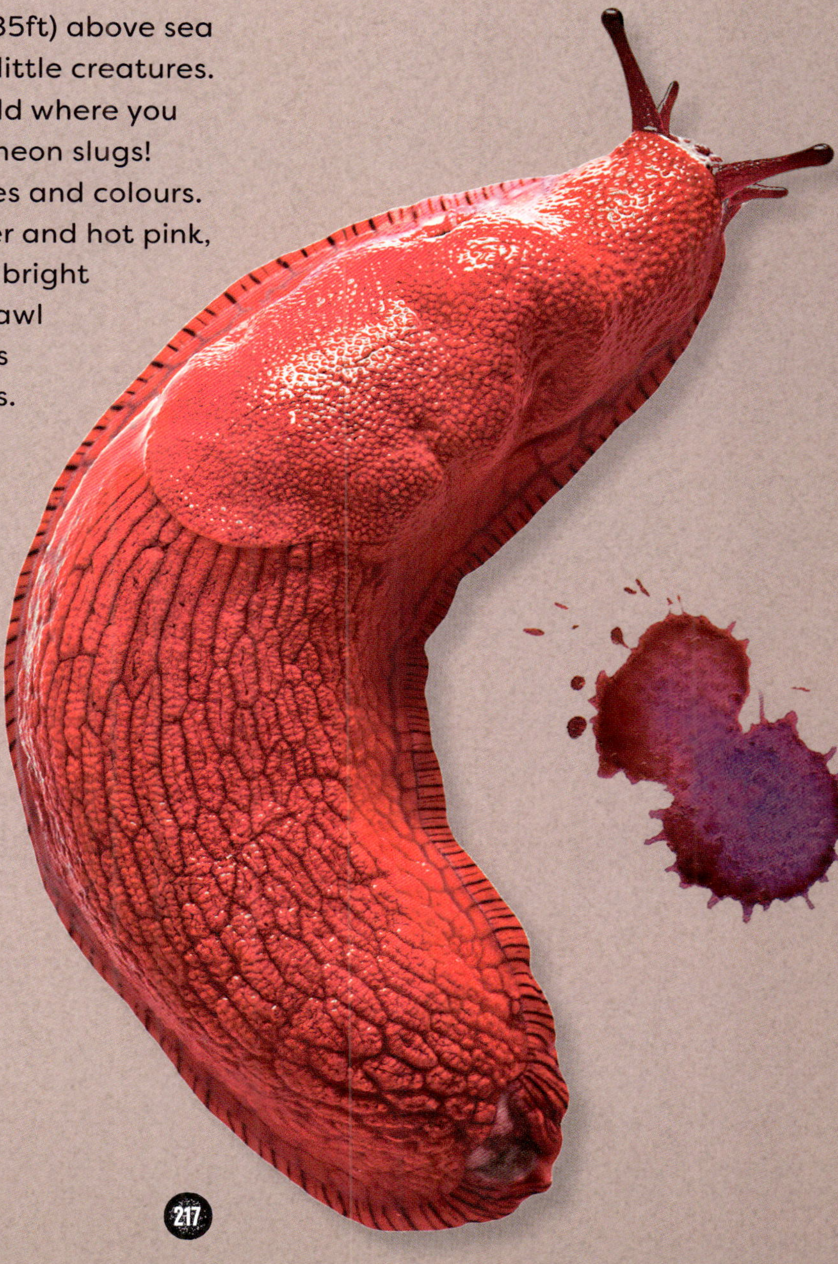

LONGITUDE 60°/120°

NEW SOUTH WALES, AUSTRALIA

SS AYRFIELD

LONGITUDE 120°/180°

It's hard to recognise that this floating island is actually a ship. The SS Ayrfield was built in 1911 and played an important role in World War II, delivering supplies to US troops stationed in the Pacific.

It was retired from service in 1972 and sent to Homebush Bay to be broken up for parts. Instead it was left to languish on the water. Over the last 50 years, the ship has been completely taken over by nature, so much so that now an entire forest has grown aboard the ship! You can barely see the rusting body beneath the greenery. Eventually the mangroves will pull the ship apart at its seams. Not even a sturdy ship that survived a war can survive a battle with nature.

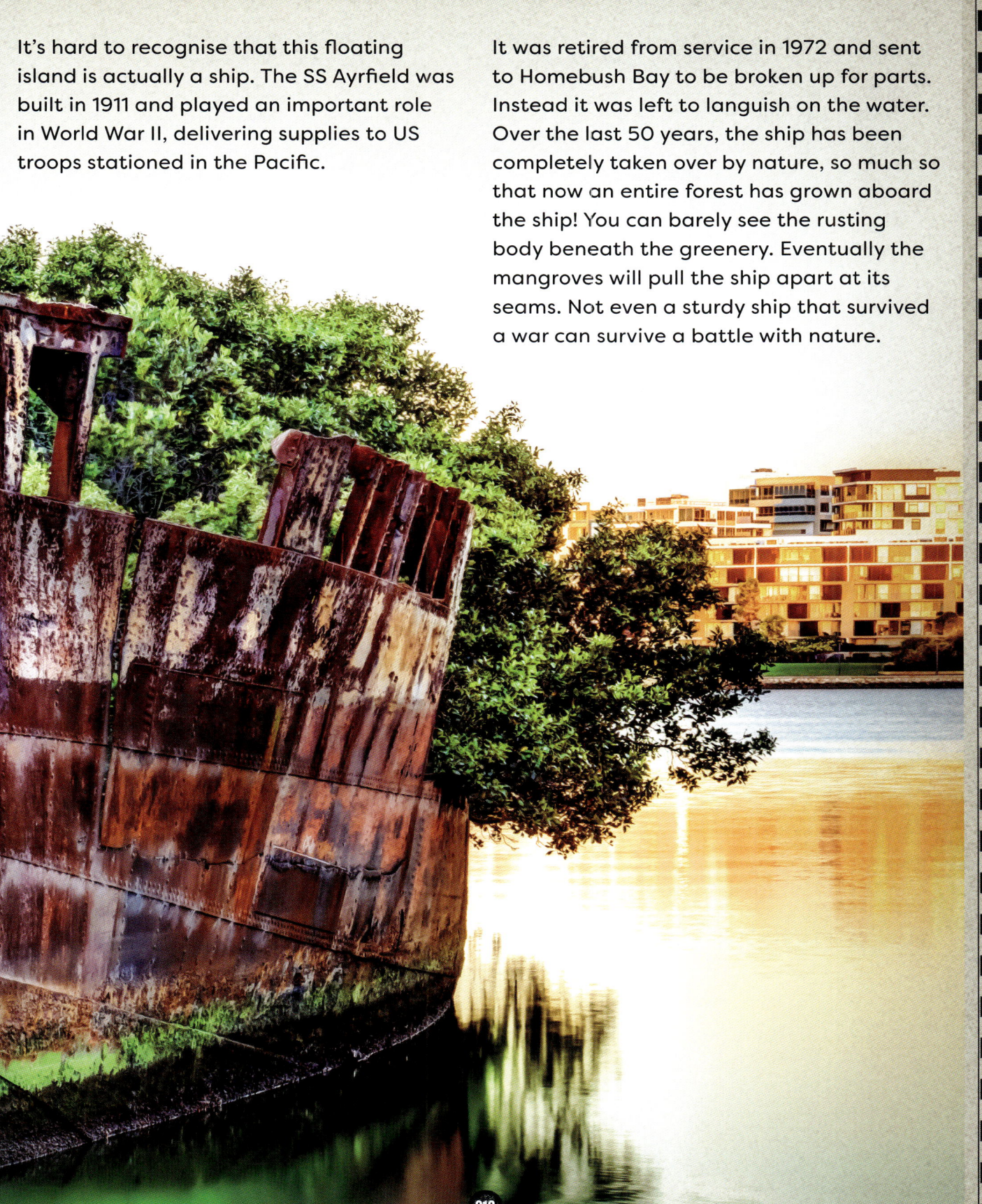

KAMCHATKA PENINSULA, RUSSIA

VALLEY OF GEYSERS

Journeying to the Kamchatka Peninsula on Russia's far-flung eastern reaches is like entering another planet. The 8km (5mi) valley stretches towards Japan, and is fed by the mega-heat of the Kikhpinych stratovolcano, a volcano that's made up of alternate layers of lava and ash.

Not only that: the Valley of Geysers looks like it's smoking. But it's not fire – it's steam puffing into the cold air. Along one narrow creek, the volcanic gases are so thick that they can kill animals and birds that get too close.

LONGITUDE 120°/180°

GRANDE TERRE, NEW CALEDONIA

HEART OF VOH

LONGITUDE 120°/180°

The mangrove trees that grow on New Caledonia's main island of Grande Terre must really love each other. Over the last two centuries, the mangrove swamp has naturally grown in the shape of a perfect heart that can be viewed from the air. Visitors in the mood for romance can take an ultralight aircraft for a flyover. The flight gives new meaning to the phrase 'love is in the air'.

HIDEAWAY ISLAND, VANUATU

UNDERWATER POST OFFICE

Did you know it's possible to post a letter while scuba diving? The postbox is stationed underwater in a marine sanctuary just off the shore of Hideaway Island. You can swim 3m (10ft) down and drop off a waterproof postcard marked with an inkless stamp. Every day, a scuba-diving postal worker collects the mail. Dogs don't bother these postal workers, but they've got a slightly bigger worry – having to fend off curious reef sharks!

LONGITUDE 120°/180°

SOUTHLAND DISTRICT, NEW ZEALAND
SLOPE POINT

Standing on rugged cliffs on the southern edge of New Zealand's South Island, these curiously shaped trees are testament to the power of nature in this exposed, blustery spot. Sculpted over the years by relentless winds blowing from the Antarctic Ocean, this small cluster of trees has grown sideways, the branches permanently twisted northwards, in the direction of the icy gusts. The powerful Antarctic winds travel uninterrupted for thousands of kilometres before hitting the coastline at Slope Point with all their might. Luckily for local farmers, the trees provide a welcome windbreak for herds of sheep that graze in the nearby fields!

A signpost at the point highlights that it is the most southerly point in New Zealand and marks the distance to the South Pole.

LONGITUDE 120°/180°

PENTECOST ISLAND, VANUATU

LAND DIVERS
OF PENTECOST ISLAND

If you think bungee jumping is wild, you haven't heard of the people who invented it. The young men of Pentecost Island start by building wooden towers in April each year. They carefully measure platform heights and test the sturdiness of the trees and vines they use. When the structures are ready, the young men climb to the top, tie a liana vine around each of their ankles, and jump. All that careful measuring means that each jumper's head barely grazes the ground!

These young men are called land divers, and this ancient ritual has been going on for centuries. Participants believe it ensures a fruitful yam harvest.

LONGITUDE 60°/120°

The towers are made using wood from the forest and are 20–30m (65–100ft) high. After each dive, the soil at the foot of the tower is raked with long sticks to create a soft landing for the next jumper.

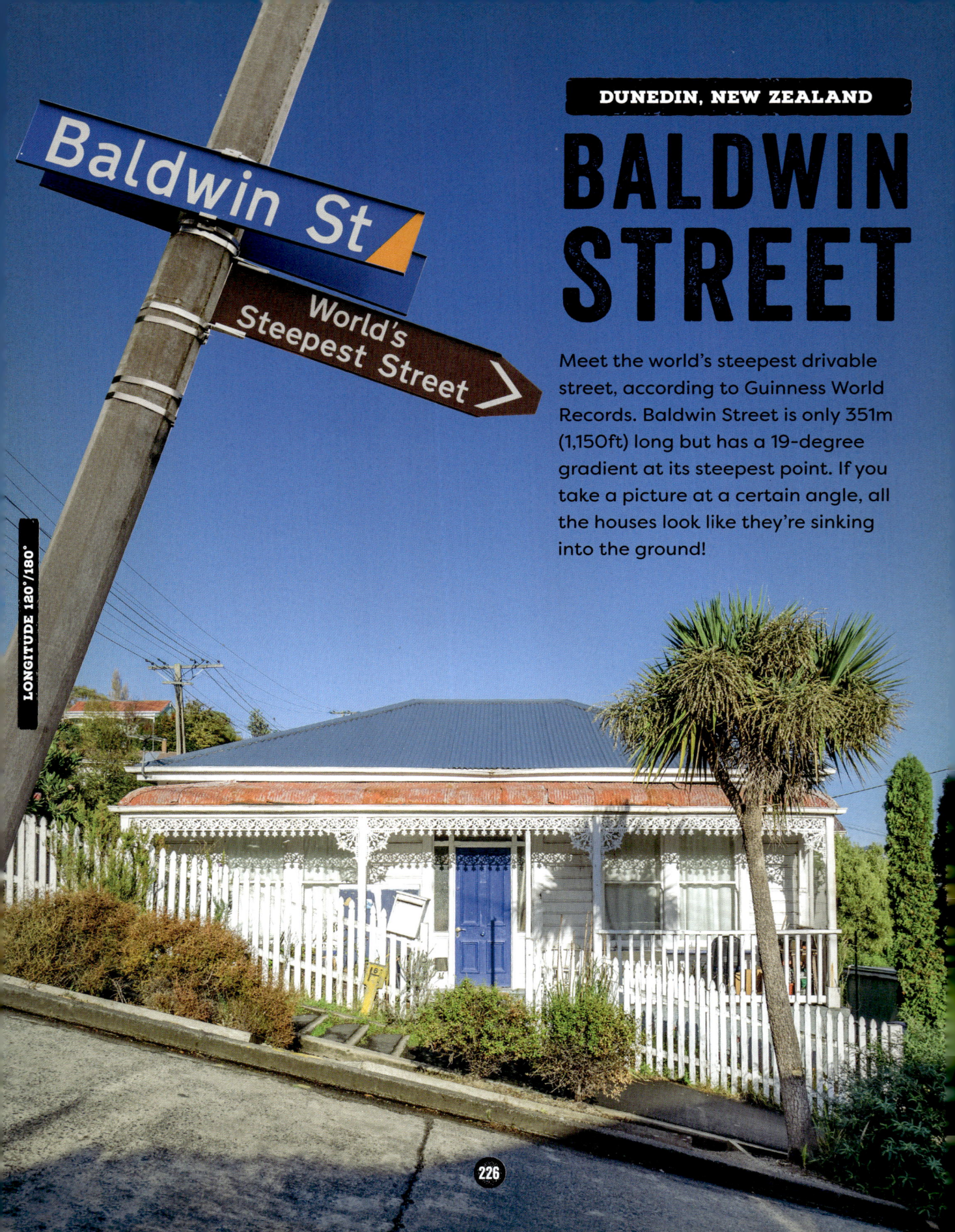

DUNEDIN, NEW ZEALAND
BALDWIN STREET

Meet the world's steepest drivable street, according to Guinness World Records. Baldwin Street is only 351m (1,150ft) long but has a 19-degree gradient at its steepest point. If you take a picture at a certain angle, all the houses look like they're sinking into the ground!

LONGITUDE 120°/180°

HOKITIKA, NEW ZEALAND
WILDFOODS FESTIVAL

In the mood for some earthworm sushi? How about pigs' trotters, lambs' tails or chocolate-covered beetles? You can find all that and more at this annual festival celebrating the unique local wild foods and flavours of the West Coast in New Zealand. Munch on cockroaches served in cups of pink jelly, wasp larvae ice cream or mountain oysters (another name for sheep testicles).

Among the delicacies on offer are huhu grubs, a type of beetle larvae, which are collected from rotten logs that are chopped up on site.

NEW ZEALAND
KĀPITI ISLAND NATURE RESERVE

New Zealand's isolation in the vast South Pacific Ocean meant that its wildlife developed in its own special way. As there were very few natural predators, many of its birds evolved to be flightless. Some grew to giant proportions, such as the now extinct moa bird, which stood up to 3.6m (12ft) tall. But with the arrival of human settlers from the 14th century onwards and the introduction of mammals, such as goats, stoats, rats, cats, possums and sheep, many of the native species began to die out.

Thankfully for nature lovers, after Kāpiti became a bird sanctuary and mammals eliminated from the island, its rare bird population made a miraculous comeback! One of the great success stories is the thriving population of little-spotted kiwis. These fuzzy, ground-dwelling birds with long beaks had almost become extinct but were brought back from the brink when five birds were transferred to Kāpiti in 1912. There are now more than 1,000 of them on the island, shuffling quietly through the forest as they forage for food.

LONGITUDE 120°/180°

WAI-O-TAPU, NEW ZEALAND
CHAMPAGNE POOL

Māori for 'sacred waters', Wai-O-Tapu is a wonderland of geothermal activity in the Lake Taupo volcanic zone. Boiling mud bubbles and pops at Mud Pool. Jets of boiling steam and water are thrust up to 20m (65ft) into the air at Lady Knox Geyser. Then there's Devil's Bath – so named because of its luminous green, toxic sulphur water. At Champagne Pool, a hot spring fizzes with carbon dioxide bubbles – just like a glass of champagne (below).

Geothermal sites such as these have been an important part of Māori culture for hundreds of years. Māori people regard these resources as *taonga* (treasures) gifted from *atua* (gods and spirits) and traditionally used the heated waters for cooking and preserving food, washing and bathing, and heating their homes. They are also used for medicinal purposes and in spiritual ceremonies.

LONGITUDE 120°/180°

WAITOMO, NEW ZEALAND

WAITOMO GLOWWORM CAVES

New Zealand is bursting with natural marvels, but these caves may just be the most marvellous of them all. As you float down the underground Waitomo River you'll enter a glow-in-the-dark wonderland. Inside are thousands of tiny glowworms emitting a dazzling turquoise light. The 'worms' are actually fungus gnats that thrive in damp, dark places. During their larval stages they become luminescent to attract prey into their sticky silky threads, producing the coolest light show on Earth (or below it).

This spectacular glowworm grotto has long been a special place to the local Māori people. According to their legends, the intricate passages were carved by powerful supernatural beings called *taniwa*. The *taniwa* continue to watch over and fiercely protect the caves, so visitors should be sure to respect them!

LONGITUDE 120°/180°

HAWKE'S BAY, NEW ZEALAND

TAUMATAWHAKATA-TANGIHANGAKOAU-AUOTAMATEATURI-PUKAKAPIKIMAUN-GAHORONUKUPOKAI-WHENUAKITANATAHU

LONGITUDE 120°/180°

At 85 letters long, Taumata Hill (as it's known by locals) has been listed by Guinness World Records as the longest place name in the world. As the legend goes, the great Māori explorer Tamatea fought a battle on the hill. His beloved brother died in the clash, and Tamatea mourned his death by playing a *kōauau* (a Māori flute) on the hill. The long name translates to 'The summit where Tamatea, the man with the big knees, the slider, climber of mountains, the land-swallower who travelled about, played his nose flute to his loved one.' Okay... now you try saying it!

INDEX

A
Actun Tunichil Muknal 43
Am Phu Cave 181
Aniakchak National Monument & Preserve 12
animals
  Bat Migration 142
  Cat Island 216
  Giant Pink Slugs of Mt Kaputar 217
  Jellyfish Lake 206
  Jigokudani Monkey Park 214
  Karni Mata Temple 160
  Komodo Dragons 191
  Nara Park 201
  Osun Sacred Forest 106
  Pig Beach 54
  Pigeon Towers 149
  Polar Bear Capital of the World (The) 40
  Red Crab Migration 178
  Snake Island 79
  Waitomo Glowworm Caves 230
  Whale Valley (Wadi Al-Hitan) 144
  Wichita Mountains Wildlife Refuge 42
  Wild Horses of the Namib Desert 125
Antarctica 73
Antogo Fishing Frenzy 96
art
  Cliff Dwellings of the Bandiagara 95
  Coral Castle 51
  Dock of Souls 62
  Fusterlandia 48
  Haw Par Villa 172
  Injalak Hill, West Arnhem Land 210
  Kelpies (The) 94
  Nine Mile Canyon 35
  Owl House 134
  Rock Paintings of Parque Nacional Serra da Capivara 82
  Wave Organ (The) 25
  Whistler Train Wreck Site 24
  Witches' Hill 130
  Witches' Market 65
  Želízy Devil Heads 120
Arulmigu Sri Rajakaliamman 168
Australia 178, 188, 195, 196, 208, 210, 211, 217, 218

B
Bahamas (The) 54
Baldwin Sreet 226
Bat & Al Ayn Tombs 153
Bat Migration 142
Bayterek Monument 159
beaches
  Hidden Beach 37
  Papakōlea Beach 18
  Pig Beach 54
  Playa de Gulpiyuri 90
  Star-Sand Beaches 203
  Tanks of Flamenco Beach 67
Belize 43
Beneficial Microbes Museum 199
Benin 103
Blue Ice Caves 83
boats
  SS *Ayrfield* 218
Bolivia 65, 66, 68
Botswana 135
Brazil 76, 78, 79, 80, 82
Bulgaria 131, 132

C
California's Lost Coast 22
Cambodia 173, 176
Campanile di Curon 111
Canada 20, 24, 30, 40, 77
Catacombes de Paris 104
Catedral de Sal 58
Cat Island 216
Cave of the Crystals 38
caves
  Actun Tunichil Muknal 43
  Am Phu Cave 181
  Blue Ice Caves 83
  Cave of the Crystals 38
  Cueva del Milodon Natural Monument 60
  Fingal's Cave 86
  Gruta do Lago Azul 76
  La Cueva del Esplendor 55
  Les Grottes Pétrifiantes 102
  Longyou Caves 187
  Postojna Caves 122
  Waitomo Glowworm Caves 230
Cayman Islands 50
Cementerio de Trenes 66
cemeteries
  Pu'upiha Cemetery 16
  Sleepy Hollow Cemetery 59
Champagne Pool 229
Chile 36, 60, 62
China 166, 170, 186, 187, 200, 201, 204
Chouara Leather Tannery 88
Cliff Dwellings of the Bandiagara 95
Colombia 55, 56, 58
Colosseum Hypogeum 116
Coober Pedy 208
Coral Castle 51
Costa Rica 45, 47
Creepy-Crawly Markets 174
Croatia 121
Crooked Forest 119
Cuba 48
Cueva del Milodón Natural Monument 60
Czechia 120

D

Darvaza Gas Crater 154
Deception Island 73
Democratic Republic of
   Congo 141
Denmark 113, 114
Derinkuyu 146
Diquís Spheres 47
Dock of Souls 62
Dragon Blood Trees 150
Drina River House 129

E

Echo Valley Hanging
   Coffins 194
Ecuador 52
Egungun Vodún Ceremony 109
Egypt 144
El Peñón de Guatapé 56
England 98

F

Fairy Forts 85
Felled Golden Spruce (The) 20
Fiji 10
Fingal's Cave 86
Finland 137
Flaming Cliffs 169
Fly Ranch Geyser 31
Forest of Knives (The) 148
forests
   Crooked Forest 119
   Forest of Knives (The) 148
   Osun Sacred Forest 106
   Submerged Forest 91
France 102, 104, 107
Fusterlandia 48
Fuxian Lake 170

G

Gambia 84
Garma Festival 211
geoglyphs
   Blythe Geoglyphs 34
   Nazca Lines 57

Gereja Ayam 184
Germany 113
geysers
   Fly Ranch Geyser 31
   Valley of Geysers 220
Ghana 97
ghost towns
   Houtouwan 200
Giant Pink Slugs of
   Mt Kaputar 217
Giant Pumpkin Regatta (The) 26
Global Seed Vault 126
Gnomesville 188
Grande Mosquée 92
Gruta do Lago Azul 76
Gunung Padang 180

H

Haenyeo 202
Haw Par Villa 172
Heart of Voh 221
Heaven Lake 204
Hell 50
Hidden Beach 37
Hill of Crosses 133
Houtouwan 200
Hunga Tonga-Hunga Ha'apai 11

I

Iceland 83
India 160, 164
Indonesia 180, 184, 190, 191, 213
Injalak Hill, West Arnhem Land
   210
Iran 149, 152
Ireland 85
islands
   Cat Island 216
   Deception Island 73
   Houtouwan 200
   Hunga Tonga-Hunga
     Ha'apai 11
   Kāpiti Island Nature Reserve
     228
   Kiritimati 15

   Kubu Island 135
   Olkhon Island 177
   Snake Island 79
   Socotra Island 150
Italy 111, 116, 117, 118, 124

J

Japan 203, 207, 214, 216
Jellyfish Lake 206
Jigokudani Monkey Park 214

K

Kaleto Fortress 131
Kane Kwei Coffins 97
Kāpiti Island Nature Reserve
   228
Karni Mata Temple 160
Kazakhstan 159, 162, 163
Kbal Spean 176
Kelpies (The) 94
Kiribati 15
Kiritimati 15
Kjeragbolten 108
Komodo Dragons 191
Korowai Tree Houses 213
Kubu Island 135
Kummakivi 137
Kyaiktiyo Pagoda 165

L

La Cueva del Esplendor 55
Lake Ballard 195
Lake Hillier 196
Lake Kaindy 163
lakes
   Campanile Di Curon 111
   Fuxian Lake 170
   Heaven Lake 204
   Lake Ballard 195
   Lake Hillier 196
   Lake Kaindy 163
   Plitvice Lakes National
     Park 121
   Spotted Lake 30

Land Divers of Pentecost Island 224
L'Anse aux Meadows 77
Le Palais Idéal 107
Les Grottes Pétrifiantes 102
Lithuania 130, 133
Living Fires 136

M
Madagascar 148
Mail Rail (The) 98
Malaysia 168
Maldives (The) 161
Mali 92, 95, 96
Mammoth Rubbing Rocks 23
Matobo National Park 138
Meghalaya Tree Bridges 164
Mexico 37, 38
Micronesia 212
Miniatur Wunderland 110
Mongolia 169
Montserrat (UK) 70
Moonhole (The) 72
Moray 61
Morocco 88
mountains
   Rainbow Mountains 166
Museo del Cerebro 53
museums
   Beneficial Microbes Museum 199
   Mail Rail (The) 98
   Museo del Cerebro 53
Myanmar (Burma) 165
My Son 182

N
Namibia 125
Nara Park 201
Navel of the World (The) 36
Nazca Lines 57
New Caledonia 221
New Zealand 223, 226, 227, 228, 229, 230, 232
Nigeria 106

Nine Mile Canyon 35
North Korea 204
North Korean Submarine 205
Norway 108, 109, 126
Nyiragongo 141

O
Old Car City 44
Olkhon Island 177
Oman 153
Osun Sacred Forest 106
Owl House 134

P
Pakistan 158
Palau 206
Pamukkale Hierapolis 140
Papakōlea Beach 18
Parque Cretácico 68
Parque Francisco Alvarado 45
Parque Nacional dos Lençóis Maranhenses 80
Passetto di Borgo 117
Peru 53, 57, 61, 64
Philippines 194
Pig Beach 54
Pigeon Towers 149
Pineapple Garden Maze 14
Playa de Gulpiyuri 90
Plitvice Lakes National Park 121
Poland 119
Polar Bear Capital of the World (The) 40
Postojna Caves 122
Princess of Hope 158
Puerto Rico 67
Pu'upiha Cemetery 16
Pyramids of Meroë 145

Q
Q-Eswachaka Rope Bridge 70

R
Råbjerg Mile 114
Racetrack Playa 33

Rafflesia Flower 190
Rainbow Eucalyptus Trees 17
Rainbow Mountains 166
Rainbow Village 198
Rai Stones 212
Red Crab Migration 178
religious sites
   Arulmigu Sri Rajakaliamman 168
   Catedral de Sal 62
   Gereja Ayam 184
   Grande Mosquée 94
   Hill of Crosses 133
   Karni Mata Temple 160
   Kbal Spean 176
   Kyaiktiyo Pagoda 165
   Matobo National Park 138
   My Son 182
   Spirit Houses 19
   Spotted Lake 30
   Temple of Ta Prohm 173
Rock Paintings of Parque Nacional Serra da Capivara 82
rocks
   Diquís Spheres 47
   El Peñón de Guatapé 56
   Gunung Padang 180
   Kjeragbolten 108
   Kummakivi 137
   Les Grottes Pétrifiantes 102
   Mammoth Rubbing Rocks 23
   Matobo National Park 138
   Moonhole (The) 72
   Nine Mile Canyon 35
   Rai Stones 212
   Rock Paintings of Parque Nacional Serra da Capivara 82
   Senegambian Stone Circles 84
   Stob Pyramids 132
   Trolltunga 109
   Vale da Lua 78
   Wolfberg Arch 128

Romania 136
Russia 177, 220

S
Scotland 86, 94
sculpture, see art
Sea of Stars (The) 161
Senegal & Gambia 84
Senegambian Stone Circles 84
Serbia 129
Shoe Tree (The) 32
Singapore 172
Singing Dunes of Altyn-Emel
  National Park 162
Sleepy Hollow Cemetery 59
Slope Point 223
Slovenia 122
Snake Island 79
Socotra Island 150
Soufrière Hills Volcano 70
South Africa 128, 134
South Korea 202, 205
Spain 90
Spirit Houses 19
Spotted Lake 30
SS *Ayrfield* 218
Star-Sand Beaches 203
Stob Pyramids 132
Stromboli 124
St Vincent & the Grenadines 72
Submerged Forest 91
Sudan 145
Sunken City of Biaie (The) 118
Swing at the End of the
  World (The) 52
Switzerland 112

T
Taiwan 198, 199
Tanks of Flamenco Beach 67
Tank Town USA 46
Taumatawhakatangihanga-
  koauauotamateaturipuka
  ka-pikimaungahoronukupo
  kaiwhenuakitanatahu 232
Tektite Underwater Habitat 69
Temple of Ta Prohm 173
Thailand 174
Tollund Man 113
Tonga 11
towns
  Hell 50
  Rainbow Village 200
trains
  Cementerio de Trenes 66
  Mail Rail (The) 98
  Miniatur Wunderland 110
  Whistler Train Wreck Site 24
trees
  Felled Golden Spruce 20
  Korowai Tree Houses 211
  Meghalaya Tree Bridges 164
  Rainbow Eucalyptus Trees 17
  Shoe Tree (The) 32
  Slope Point 223
  Submerged Forest 91
Triftbrücke 112
Trolltunga 109
Turkey 140, 146
Turkmenistan 154

U
UK 70, 86, 91, 94, 98
Underwater Post Office 222
unusual buildings
  Bayterek Monument 159
  Drina River House 129
  Le Palais Idéal 107
  Pigeon Towers 149
  Winchester Mystery House 27
  Zoroastrian Towers of
    Silence 152
USA 12, 14, 16, 17, 18, 19, 22, 23,
  25, 26, 27, 31, 32, 33, 34, 35,
  42, 44, 46, 51, 59, 67, 69

V
Vale da Lua 78
Valley of Geysers 220
Vanuatu 222, 224
Vietnam 181, 182
Virgin Islands (USA) 69
volcanoes
  Aniakchak National
    Monument & Preserve 12
  Deception Island 73
  Hunga Tonga-Hunga
    Ha'apai 11
  Nyiragongo 141
  Soufrière Hills Volcano 70
  Stromboli 124

W
Wadi Al-Hitan (Whale Valley)
  144
Waitavala Water Slide 10
Waitomo Glowworm Caves 230
Wales 91
waterfalls
  Waitavala Water Slide 10
  Wave Organ (The) 25
Whistler Train Wreck Site 24
Wichita Mountains Wildlife
  Refuge 42
Wildfoods Festival 227
Wild Horses of the Namib
  Desert 125
Winchester Mystery House 27
Witches' Hill 130
Witches' Market 65
Wolfberg Arch 128

Y
Yemen 150

Z
Zambia 142
Želízy Devil Heads 120
Zhangye Danxia National
  Geopark 166
Zhengbei Tower 186
Zimbabwe 138
Zoroastrian Towers of Silence 152

PICTURE CREDITS

Cover: BlueOrange Studio/Shutterstock (jellyfish lake, and on p206); Yevheniia Lytvynovych/Shutterstock (seaweed, and t/o); Camek/Shutterstock (fish, and t/o); stasia_ch/Shutterstock (sloth, and on p74 and p76); Daniel Prudek/Shutterstock (spider geoglyph, and on p57); Yutthana Chumkhot/EyeEm/Getty (human skull, and on p101 and p104); Evgeny Turaev/Shutterstock (lion, and on p101 and p116); Morphart Creation/Shutterstock (bat, and on p100 and p142); Barandash Karandashich/Shutterstock (goblin, and on p102); Piranka/Getty (olm, and on p100 and p122); Rainer Albiez/Shutterstock (Stromboli Volcano, and on p3 and p124); Arthur Balitskii (submarine, and on p205); Croisy/Shutterstock (human brain, and on p2 and p53); vectortatu/Shutterstock (clouds and stars); Bodor Tivadar/Shutterstock (balloon); Maria Isaeva/Shutterstock (magnifying glass, and on p1); Lotus_studio/Shutterstock (compass) / p1: Niklas Moeller/Shutterstock (ice cave, and on p83); pp2-3: Evgeny Turaev/Shutterstock (bear, and on p12); Darryl Brooks/Shutterstock (Old Car City, and on p29 and p44); pixbull/Shutterstock (Moroccan shoes, and on p74 and p88); THONGCHAI.S/Shutterstock (Rainbow Mountains, and on pp166-167); imagevixen/Shutterstock (Lake Ballard, and on p195); f4 Luftbilder (Pineapple Maze, and on p14); caioacquesta/Shutterstock (golden lancehead, and on p79 and p240); Golden Shrimp/Shutterstock (Lord Shiva, and on p5 and p182); farida-tatarova/Shutterstock (paint splash) / p4: Danita Delimont/Shutterstock (rainbow eucalyptus, and on p17); arfpmbd/Shutterstock (tree, and on p91); Torsten Pursche/Shutterstock (Dogon village, and on p85) / p5: Morphart Creation/Shutterstock (tarantula, and on p157 and p174) / pp6-7: Kamran Ali/Shutterstock (Swing at the End of the World, and on p52); Barashkova Natalia/Shutterstock (ship) / p8: Gts/Shutterstock (spray can, and on p24); Uwe Bergwitz/Shutterstock (Eklutna Cemetery, and on p19); Evgeny Turaev/Shutterstock (elk, and on p22); DELstudio/Shutterstock (axe, and on p20) / p9: Anton Evseev/Shutterstock (rainbow eucalyptus, and on p17); Ilya Images/Shutterstock (Utah Great Pumpkin Regatta, and on p26) / p10: DruZhi Art/Shutterstock (life vest); Scott Flaherty Photograph/Shutterstock (Waitavala waterslide) / p11: Xinhua/Shutterstock (Hunga Tonga) / p12: NPC Collectiom/Alamy (Aniakchak National Monument and Preserve) / p14: vector_ann/Shutterstock (pineapple) / p15: Kyung Muk Lim/Shutterstock (Christmas Island); ArtColibris/Shutterstock (banana) / p16: Geostock/Getty; (Puupiha Cemetery) / p17: backUp/Shutterstock (tape); Masha Dav/Shutterstock (flowers) / p18: gg-foto/Shutterstock (Papakolea green sand beach) / p19: Uwe Bergwitz/Shutterstock (Eklutna Cemetery) / p20: Migren art/Shutterstock (tape measure); HAKINMHAN/Shutterstock (tree stump); maximmmmum/Shutterstock (cut tree) / p21: Pierre Longnus/getty (golden spruce) / p22: Pete Niesen/Shutterstock (cattle grazing, Lost Coast) / p23: Diane N. Ennis/Shutterstock (Mammoth Rubbing Rocks); Morphart Creation/Shutterstock (mammoth) / p24: somika87/Shutterstock (spray paint); John Crux/Shutterstock (Whistler train) / p25: Karlis Dambrans/Shutterstock (wave organ); Morphart Creation/Shutterstock (engraving) / p26: Nata_Alhontess/Shutterstock (pumpkin) / p27: DELstudio/Shutterstock (ghost); CREATISTA/Shutterstock (Winchester Mystery House) / p28: Jason Winter/Shutterstock (tank track, and on p46); Ethan Daniels/Shutterstock (chinstrap penguins, and on p73); Morphart Creation/Shutterstock (magnet, and on p36); aceshot1/Shutterstock (Churchill tundra buggy, and on p40) / p29: TravelPhotoBloggers/Shutterstock (Pig Beach, and on p54); Customdesigner/Shutterstock (shoes, and on p32) / p30: Wirestock Creators/Shutterstock (Osoyoos Spotted Lake) / p31: Morphart Creation/Shutterstock (corkscrew); Fotogro/Shutterstock (Fly Geyser) / p32: Rachid Dahnoun/Getty (shoe tree) / p33: AcantStudio/Shutterstock (rock); Facethewind/Getty (Racetrack Playa) / p34: Rsfinlayson/Wikimedia Commons (Blythe Intaglios) / p35: jnerad/Getty (Nine Mile Canyon) / p36: Ralf Hettler/Getty (Easter Island stones) / p37: Melok/Shutterstock (seashells); Ferran Traite/Getty (The Hidden Beach) / p38: Alexander Van Driessche/Wikimedia Commons (cave of the crystals) / p40: Sergey Uryadnikov/Shutterstock (polar bear and cubs); Bildagentur Zoonar GmbH/Shutterstock (polar bear/tundra buggy) / p42: Zack Frank/Shutterstock (bison) / p43: taviphoto/Shutterstock (bones); David Lazenby/Alamy (Maya skeleton) / p44: Darryl Brooks/Shutterstock (Old Car City); Darryl Brooks/Shutterstock (Old Car City); Darryl Brooks/Shutterstock (Old Car City) / p45: Galyna Andrushko/Shutterstock (Park Francisco Alvarado); Bodor Tivadar/Shutterstock (garden pruner) / p46: MaKars/Shutterstock (tank); Jason Winter/Shutterstock (tyre tracks); Joerg Huettenhoelscher/Shutterstock (tank crushing car) / p47: Inspired By Maps/Shutterstock (Diquis spheres) / p48: Anne-Marie Palmer/Alamy (Fusterlandia) / p50: jumpingsack/Shutterstock (monster); Hank Shiffman/Shutterstock (Hell) / p51: BorisVetshev/Shutterstock (Coral Castle) / p52: Kamran Ali/Shutterstock (Swing at the End of the World) / p53: MriMan/Shutterstock (MRI scan); gmstockstudio/Shutterstock (MRI scan) / p54: Nata_Alhontess/Shutterstock (palm tree); Bodor Tivadar/Shutterstock (umbrella); TravelPhotoBloggers/Shutterstock (Pig Beach) / p55: Ekatmarts/Shutterstock (hiking boots, and on p128); Gilles Barbier/Getty (Cueva del Esplendor) / p56: Fotos593/Shutterstock (El Penon); Arthur Balitskii/Shutterstock (binoculars) / p57: StanislavBeloglazov/Shutterstock (Nazca Lines) / p58: Valentyn Volkov/Shutterstock (white rock salt); posztos/Shutterstock (Salt Cathedral Zipaquira) / p59: Vera Petruk/Shutterstock (headless horseman); Daniel M. Silva/Shutterstock (Sleepy Hollow Cemetery) / p60: Dario Sabljak/Shutterstock (Smilodon skull); Erlantz P.R/Shutterstock Cueva del Milodon Natural Monument / p61: Morphart Creation/Shutterstock (maize); ClaireMcAdams/Getty (Moray ruins) / p62: Diego Grandi/Shutterstock (Dock of Souls) / p64: Tuul & Bruno Morandi/Getty (Quechua women weaving); Joerg Steber/Shutterstock (rope bridge) / p65: Juergen Ritterbach/Alamy (La Paz Witches Market) / p66: ledokolua/Shutterstock (steam train); Vladimir Melnik/Shutterstock (Uyuni train cemetery) / p67: Bodor Tivadar/Shutterstock (sandcastle); Christian Wheatley/Getty (tank on Flamendo Beach) / p68: Wouter Roog/Shutterstock (dinosaur footprints) / p69: Bettmann/Getty (Tektite underwater habitat); Alena Ohneva/Shutterstock (air bubbles) / p70: Richard Roscoe/500pxRF (Soufriere Hills Volcano) / p72: Nikolaenko Ekaterina/Shutterstock (Moon); Aneese/Getty (Moonhole) / p73: Ethan Daniels/Shutterstock (chinstrap penguins); Achim Baque/Shutterstock (Deception Island) / p74: Hennensarg von Kudjo Affutu/Wikimedia Commons (hen coffin, and on p97 / p75: Marcos Amend/Shutterstock (Serra da Capivara National Park, and on p82) / p76: Sandro Helmann/Getty (Gruta do Lago Azul) / p77: PT Hamilton/Shutterstock (Viking village, Newfoundland); BORTEL Pavel - Pavelmidi/Shutterstock (Viking battle axe) / p78: Vitormarigo/Canto (Moon Valley) / p79: Leo Francini/Alamy (Snake Island, and on p240) / p80: Wilson Santos Marques/Shutterstock (Lençóis Maranhenses); vectortatu/Shutterstock (clouds, and t/o) / p82: Marcos Amend/Shutterstock (Serra da Capivara National Park) / p83: Niklas Moeller/Shutterstock (Vatnajökull blue ice cave) / p84: DorSteffen/Shutterstock (Senegambian Stone Circle) / p85: Declan Mcphillips/Shutterstock (Grianán of Aileach); John Duncan/Dundee Art Galleries and Museums/Wikimedia Commons ('The Riders of the Sidhe') / p86: 13threephotography/Shutterstock (Fingal's Cave); MNStudio/Shutterstock (Giant's Causeway) / p87: Steve Allen/Shutterstock (Fingal's Cave) / p88: Hyserb/Shutterstock (Chouara Tannery) / p90: barmalini/Shutterstock (Playa de Gulpiyuri) / p91: Matthew Horwood/Getty (Borth submerged forest) / p92: David MG (The Great Mosque of Djenné); Quick Shot/Shutterstock (Djenné market crowd) / p94: VicS21/Shutterstock (Kelpies) / p95: Torsten Pursche/Shutterstock (Dogon village mud buildings); Torsten Pursche/Shutterstock (Dogon cliff dwellings) / p96: Huib Blom/Alamy (Mali fishing frenzy) / p97: Jean-Michel Rousset/ Wikimedia Commons (Kane Kwei workshop) / p98: RichartPhotos/Shutterstock (Mail Rail Museum) / p100: michael nicolai/Shutterstock (lemur, and on p148); nevereverro/Getty (Kjeragbolten, and on p108) / p101: Dan Kitwood (vodun festival, and on p103) / p102: FORGET Patrick/SAGAPHOTO.COM/Alamy (petrifying caves) / p104: Heracles Kritikos/Shutterstock (Catacombs of Paris) / p106: Vladimir Wrangel/Shutterstock (Osun Forest); Africulture/Shutterstock (Osun Forest sculpture) / p107: milosk50/Shutterstock (Palais Ideal) / p109: Adobe Stock (Trolltunga) / p100: Rawpixel.com/Shutterstock (eyeglasses), Vadym_D/Shutterstock (Miniatur Wunderland) / p111: Creative Travel Projects/Shutterstock (Curon Venosta church) / p112: Kamil Kwiatkowski/Shutterstock (Triftbrücke) / p113: Tim Graham/Getty (Tollund Man) / p114: Arthur Balitskii/Shutterstock (binoculars); Pilguj/Shutterstock (white sand dunes) / p116: SCStock/Shutterstock (Colosseum, Rome); renbrins/Shutterstock (view from inside the Colosseum) / p117: Aerial-motion/Shutterstock (Castel Sant'Angelo, Rome) / p118: Antonio Busiello/Getty (Baia statue) / p119: David Johnston/Adobe Stock (Crooked Forest) / p120: AirP72/Shutterstock (Devil's Heads) / p121: Rob Zweers/ Wikimedia Commons (Alcon blue); Fesus Robert/Shutterstock (Plitvice National Park in Croatia) / p122: STUDIO MELANGE/Shutterstock (Postojna cave) / p124: Marzolino/Shutterstock (Stromboli Island old view) / p125: 2630ben/Shutterstock (wild horses) / p126: Memo Angeles/Shutterstock (zombie hand and arms); Marcin Kadziolka/Shutterstock (Global Seed Vault); HELENE DAUSCHY/Getty (Global Seed Vault boxes); Herman du Plessis/Getty (Wolfberg) / p129: Alberto Loyo/Shutterstock (Drina) / p130: Stonico/Shutterstock (witch); Yevgen Belich/Shutterstock (Witch Hill) / p131: Nataliya Nazarova/Shutterstock (Kaleto Fortress) / p132: Orit Yishai/Shutterstock (Stob Pyramids); Gencho Petkov/Shutterstock (Stob Pyramids) / p133: Gorsh13/Getty (Hill of Crosses) / p134: Vanessa Bentley/Shutterstock (Owl House); Richard van der Spuy/Shutterstock (Owl House) /p135: 2630ben/Shutterstock (Kubu Island) / p136: Marzufello/Shutterstock (fire); Roberto Sorin/Shutterstock (living fires) / p137: Esa Juusola/EyeEm/Getty (Kummakivi) / p138: Trek Bears Photography/Shutterstock (Matobo National Park); Malgorzata Drewniak/Shutterstock (rainbow lizard) / p140: Suksamran1985/Shutterstock (Pamukkale) / p141: Arthur Balitskii/Shutterstock (volcano sketch); Marian Galovic/Shutterstock (Nyiragongo volcano) / p142: Fabian von Poser/Getty (fruit bats in flight) / p144: AhmedMosaad/Wikimedia Commons (Whale Valley) / p145: evenfh/Shutterstock (Meroe) / p146: Brester Irina/Shutterstock (Cappadocia, Turkey); frantic00/Getty (fairy chimneys in Cappadocia) / p148: Pierre-Yves Babelon/Getty (Tsingy de Bemaraha) / p149: Mazzzur/Getty (pigeon towers, exterior); Poliorketes/Shutterstock (pigeon tower, interior) / p150: Mario Eder/Getty (Socotra Island); Vectonessa/Shutterstock (blood drip) / p152: Fotokon/Shutterstock (Towers of Silence) / p153: ZambeziShark/Getty (Beehive Tombs, close-up); Kylie Nicholson/Shutterstock (Beehive Tombs) / p154: Thiago B Trevisan/Shutterstock (Darvaza Gas Crater) / 156: Kiratsinh Jadeja/Getty (idol of Ganesha, and on p168); Norman Ong/Shutterstock (Rafflesia flower, and on p190); Kseniakrop/Shutterstock (garden gnome, and on p188) / p157: Ipsita Ghosh/Shutterstock (Karni Mata Temple, and on p160); Maks08/Getty (Am Phu Cave sculpture, and on p181) / p158: only_vector/Shutterstock (desert mountains); SM Rafiq Photography/Getty (Princess of Hope) / p159: evgenykz/Shutterstock (Bayterek Tower) / p160: Novarc Images/Alamy (Karni Mata Temple ceremony) / p161: nabyh/Shutterstock (bioluminescent beach) / p162: Temir Shintemirov/Shutterstock (Altyn Emel National Park) / p163: Humancode/Getty (Lake Kaindy) / p164: WanderDream/Shutterstock (Meghalaya) / p165: MOLPIX/Shutterstock (Golden Rock, Kyaiktiyo) / p166: THONGCHAI.S/Shutterstock (Rainbow Mountains); p167: Ana Flasker/Shutterstock (Rainbow Mountains) / p168: Tanukiphoto/Getty (Arulmigu Sri RajaKaliamman temple) / p169: Daniel Karfik/Shutterstock (Flaming Cliffs); Daniel Andis/Shutterstock (dinosaur eggs) / p170: HelloRF Zcool/Shutterstock (Fuxian Lake) / p172: Phil Weymouth/Lonely Planet Traveller Magazine (seals, Haw Par Villa); Matt Munro/Lonely Planet Traveller Magazine (characters, Haw Par Villa); Sivarock/Getty (dragon, Haw Par Villa) / p173: Framalicious/Shutterstock (Ta Prohm temple) / p174: Jan Jenka/Shutterstock (fried spiders); p176: Noppasin Wongchum/Getty (Kbal Spean) / p177: Katvic/Shutterstock (Lake Baikal); Alexandru Nika/Shutterstock (shamanic tree) / p178: Juergen Freund/Nature Picture Library (Christmas Island crabs) / p179: WaterFrame/Alamy (juvenile crabs) / p180: Rawpixel.com/Shutterstock (Gunung Padang) / p181: saiko3p/Getty (marble mountains) / p182: Golden Shrimp/Shutterstock (Lord Shiva); Roman Babakin (My Son temple) / p183: Chonlawut/Shutterstock (My Son engraving) / p184: Sony Herdiana/Shutterstock (Chicken Church) / p186: Dawn Minkow/Shutterstock (Zhengbeilou Tower) / p187: Jianhua Qiu (Longyou caves) / p188: becauz gao/Shutterstock (Gnomesville) / p191: USO/Getty (Komodo dragons) / p192: Bodor Tivadar/Shutterstock (coffin, and on p194); TravelPhotoBloggers/Shutterstock (snow monkeys, and on p214); grebcha/Shutterstock (bacteria, and on p199); koi88/Shutterstock (star sand, and on p203) / p193: Yevheniia Lytvynov/Shutterstock (coral, and on p222); Chansom Pantip/Shutterstock (ivy, and on p200); Eli Duke/Wikimedia Commons (huhu grub, and on p227); Milano M/Shutterstock (paint splatter, and on p198) / p194: raphme/Shutterstock (hanging coffins) / p195: imagevixen/Shutterstock (Lake Ballard) / p196: matteo_it/Shutterstock (Lake Hillier) / p198: Michael Gordon/Shutterstock (Rainbow Village) / DELstudio/Shutterstock (microscope); farida-tatarova/Shutterstock (paint) / p200: Joe Nafis/Shutterstock (Houtouwan) / p201: eva_mask/Shutterstock (deer); ItzaVU/Shutterstock (Nara Park) / p202: Bodor Tivadar/Shutterstock (sea urchin) / KIM WONKOOK/Shutterstock (haenyeo) / p203: leungchopan/Shutterstock (Kabira Bay) / p204: Fcloud/Shutterstock (monster); Sofiaworld/Shutterstock (Lake Tianchi) / p205: aminkorea/Shutterstock (North Korean submarine) / p206: Shalamov/Getty (golden jellyfish) / p208: Torsten Pursche/Shutterstock (Coober Pedy) / p209: Adwo/Shutterstock (opal seam) / Alexandre.ROSA/Shutterstock (Coober Pedy kitchen) / p210: Sarah Reid/Lonely Planet (Injalak Hill) / p211: J Mundy/Shutterstock (Yolngu dancers) / p212: Stephen B. Goodwin/Shutterstock (stamps); RobNaw/Shutterstock (Rai stones) / p213: GUDKOV ANDREY/Shutterstock (Korowai) / p214: norikko/Shutterstock (snowballs) / p216: Bodor Tivadar/Shutterstock (cat) / Sankei/Getty (Tashirojima Island) / p217: Emmanuel LATTES/Alamy (slug) / farida-tatarova/Shutterstock (paint) / p218: Benny Marty/Shutterstock SS Ayrfield / p220: by Alla/Shutterstock (Valley of Geysers) / p221: cachou44/Getty (Voh) / p222: AFP/Getty (post office) / p223: Gabor Kovacs Photography/Shutterstock (Slope Point); Phillip Richter/Getty (Slope Point sign) / p224: Pvince73/Shutterstock (Vanuatu) / p226: gracethang2/Shutterstock (Baldwin Street); Umomos/Shutterstock (Baldwin Street sign) / p227: Kai Schwoerer/Getty (Hokitika Wildfoods) / p228: JohnCarnemolla/Getty (kiwi); CLRgraphics/Shutterstock (Kapiti Island) / p229: Christopher Chan/Getty (Champagne Pool) / p230: Shaun Jeffers/Shutterstock (Waitomo) / p232: Martin Vlnas/Shutterstock (Te Mata Peak) /p239: Alex Rockheart/Shutterstock (camera)

ACKNOWLEDGMENTS

Publishing Director: Piers Pickard / Publisher: Rebecca Hunt
Editorial Director: Joe Fullman / Editor: Kate Baker / Author: Nicole Maggi
Additional Text: Kate Baker / Art Director: Andy Mansfield / Print Production: Nigel Longuet

Published in March 2026 by Lonely Planet Global Limited
CRN: 554153 / ISBN: 978-1-83758-873-2
www.lonelyplanet.com/kids
© Lonely Planet 2026
2 4 6 8 10 9 7 5 3 1
Printed in Malaysia

All rights reserved. No part of this publication may be reproduced, stored in a retrieval system, or transmitted in any form by any means, electronic, mechanical, photocopying, recording, or otherwise, except brief extracts for the purpose of review, without the written permission of the publisher. Lonely Planet and the Lonely Planet logo are trademarks of Lonely Planet and are registered in the US Patent and Trademark Office and in other countries.

Although the author and Lonely Planet have taken all reasonable care in preparing this book, we make no warranty about the accuracy or completeness of its content and, to the maximum extent permitted, disclaim all liability from its use.

STAY IN TOUCH - lonelyplanet.com/contact

IRELAND Digital Depot, Roe Lane (off Thomas St), Digital Hub, Dublin 8, D08 TCV4, Ireland

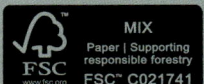

Paper in this book is certified against the Forest Stewardship Council™ standards. FSC™ promotes environmentally responsible, socially beneficial and economically viable management of the world's forests.